Making Budgets Work

The control and use
of the
budgetary control process

Professor Douglas Garbutt
PhD, MEd, FCMA, ACIS, AcDipEd

Contents

Acknowledgements

Abstract

1 General Considerations: An Introduction to Budgeting

1.1	Budget definition	1
1.2	Budgetary control	1
1.3	Budget statements	1
1.4	Values, price and quantity	1
1.5	Prior preparation and approval	2
1.6	Strategic budgets	2
1.7	Objectives	2
1.8	Management information	2
1.9	Performance monitoring and evaluation.	2
1.10	Capital expenditure budgeting	2
1.11	The role of the management accountant	3

2 Administration of the Budgetary Process   5

2.1	Leadership	5
2.2	Starting to build the budgeting system	5
2.3	Budgeting stages	6
2.4	Budget purposes	7
2.5	Budget structure	7
2.6	Business strategy, planning and objectives	7
2.7	Business objectives	8
2.8	Financial objectives	8
2.9	Operating objectives	8
2.10	Clear and measurable objectives	8
2.11	Key budget factors	8
2.12	Budget centres	9
2.13	Types of budget centre	9
2.14	Controllable costs and revenues	10
2.15	Flexible budget comparisons	10
2.16	Budget period	10
2.17	Natural business year	11
2.18	Seasonal factors	11
2.19	Control period	11
2.20	Calendarisation	11
2.21	Continuous and rolling budgets	11
2.22	Flexible budgets and accounting policies	12
2.23	Operating budgets	12

2.24 Service department budgets 12
2.25 Principal budget factor 12
2.26 Master budget 12
2.27 Centralisation versus decentralisation 13
2.28 Integrated control systems 13
2.29 Preparing a draft budget 14
2.30 Tasks, objectives and information in budget preparation 15
2.31 Setting the budget timetable 16
2.32 Completion time 16
2.33 Starting time 16
2.34 Budgets required by group or parent companies 16
2.35 Group/parent objectives 17
2.36 Market trends and competition 17
2.37 Relation to strategic plans 17
2.38 Budgets for subsidiaries 17
2.39 Tax planning and treasury function 18
2.40 Budget timetable for a group 18
2.41 Developing the budget manual 19
2.42 Contents of the budget manual 19
2.43 Classification and coding of accounts 20

3 Financial Objectives and Budgets

21

3.1 The key role of financial objectives in budgeting 21
3.2 The financial budgets 21
3.3 Contents of financial budgets 22
3.4 Two levels of financial planning 22
3.5 Importance of marketing plans 22
3.6 Deciding business objectives 23
3.7 Influences on business objectives 23
3.8 Examples of business objectives 23
3.9 Financial budget objectives 24
3.10 Ways of expressing objectives 25
3.11 Profit and loss account and balance sheet measures 25
3.12 Board to set objectives 26
3.13 Departmental, functional and product objectives 26
3.14 Preparing budget guidelines 26
3.15 Pro forma financial statements 27
3.16 Need for standard definitions 27
3.17 The profit and loss statements 27
3.18 The balance sheet 31

4 Preparing Income Budgets

37

4.1 Priority of sales budgets 37
4.2 Basis of the income budgets 37

4.3	Relation to strategic income budget	38
4.4	The sales plan	38
4.5	Marketing targets	39
4.6	Targets for sales	39
4.7	Product sales targets	39
4.8	Target volumes and prices	40
4.9	Cost, asset and profit targets	40
4.10	Funding targets	41
4.11	Marketing strategy	41
4.12	Defining the market(s) for the company's products	41
4.13	Market segments	42
4.14	Marketing policy	43
4.15	Differential advantage	43
4.16	The marketing mix	43
4.17	Global markets	44
4.18	Developing the product range	44
4.19	Intangible services	44
4.20	New products	45
4.21	Product viability	45
4.22	Analysis of demand characteristics of market(s) served	46
4.23	The supply characteristics of markets served	46
4.24	Volume and market share by sector and brand	47
4.25	Pricing and sales volumes	48
4.26	Key market indicators	48
4.27	Estimating sales volumes	48
4.28	Advertising allocations	49
4.29	Brand and product leadership	49
4.30	Consumer trends, company expertise and resources	49
4.31	The marketing plan	49
4.32	The product life cycle	50
4.33	The ideal product life cycle	51
4.34	Competitive stages	51
4.35	Price and promotion spending	52
4.36	Type of sale	53
4.37	Cannibalisation	53
4.38	Records of product performance	54
4.39	Financial appraisal of new proposals	54
4.40	Financial statement for new proposals	54
4.41	Costs of new proposals	55
4.42	Price and margin analysis	56
4.43	Brand (product) volumes and market shares	56
4.44	Brand (product) prices	56
4.45	Discretionary marketing expenditure	56
4.46	Profitability analysis	57
4.47	New product contribution analysis	57
4.48	Transfer pricing	57

5 Preparing Operating and Expenditure Budgets 59

5.1 Operating and expenditure budgets 59
5.2 Changing economic environment 59
5.3 New approaches 60
5.4 The systems approach 60
5.5 Open and closed systems 60
5.6 Characteristics of a good system 61
5.7 Operating objectives 61
5.8 Operating measures 61
5.9 Determinants of outputs and inputs 62
5.10 Input and output measures in monitoring and control 63
5.11 Efficiency, economy and effectiveness 64
5.12 Fixed and variable costs 64
5.13 Variable costs 64
5.14 Component fixed costs 65
5.15 Overall fixed costs 65
5.16 Committed, programmed or managed fixed costs 66
5.17 Average fixed cost 66
5.18 Personnel costs 66
5.19 Number of people employed 67
5.20 Headcount 67
5.21 Wages, salaries and benefits 68
5.22 Employee related payments 68
5.23 An example of budgeting for a sales force 69
5.24 An example of production, engineeering and distribution objectives 70
5.25 Estimating production volume 70
5.26 Estimating production costs 71

6 Budgeting for Asset Costs 73

6.1 Asset budgets and capital budgeting 73
6.2 Purpose of asset budgets 73
6.3 Definition of assets 74
6.4 Determinants of working capital 74
6.5 Working capital budgets 75
6.6 Depreciation of fixed assets 75
6.7 Budgeting for assets coming on stream 76
6.8 Incomes from new assets 76
6.9 Depreciation on new assets 76
6.10 Maintenance costs 77
6.11 Repair and inspection costs 77
6.12 Replacements, improvements or refurbishments. 77

7 Funds Flow and Working Capital Budgets 79

7.1 Funds flow and working capital in budgeting 79

7.2 Funds flow and profits   79
7.3 The cost and value of funds   79
7.4 The treasury function   80
7.5 Risk management   80
7.6 The purpose of funds flow and working capital statements   80
7.7 When funds flow statements are prepared   81
7.8 Should you prepare funds flow or working capital statements ?   81
7.9 Categories of funds flow   82
7.10 Items in the funds flow statement   82
7.11 Items in the working capital statement   84
7.12 Net working capital   85
7.13 Funding requirements   85
7.14 Agreement with balance sheet   85
7.15 Analysis by providers of funds   86
7.16 Providers of funds   86
7.17 The funds flow budget period   86
7.18 The knock-on effect on working capital and cash balances   86
7.19 Working capital and profitability   87
7.20 The timing effects on working capital   87

8 Performance Monitoring and Control   89

8.1 Performance monitoring   89
8.2 Performance control   89
8.3 The purposes of performance monitoring and control   89
8.4 Fulfilling the business strategy   90
8.5 Establishing control points   90
8.6 How budgets control expenditure   90
8.7 Controllable costs   90
8.8 Control of profits and balance sheet   91
8.9 Control of funds flows   91
8.10 Responsibility accounting   91
8.11 Drilling down   92
8.12 Integrated control systems   92
8.13 Performance control relevance   93
8.14 Frequency of reports   93
8.15 Detail of reports   93
8.16 Timeliness   93
8.17 Need for reports and cost   94
8.18 Tasks, objectives and information in controlling budgets   94
8.19 Comparisons   95
8.20 Actual to budget comparisons   95
8.21 Cumulative figures   95
8.22 Past period comparisons   96
8.23 Combining budgets and forecasts   96
8.24 Ratios and operational comparisons   96
8.25 Long and medium-term budget comparisons   97

8.26	Inter-firm comparisons	97
8.27	Flexible budget comparisons	97
8.28	Variance accounting	98
8.29	Causes of variance	98
8.30	Short and long term variances	98
8.31	Service department variances	99
8.32	Corrective actions	99
8.33	Monitoring and reporting non-financial performance	99
8.34	Explanations and actions	100
8.35	Corrective action reports and follow-up	100
8.36	Budget review meetings	100
8.37	Reward systems	100

9 Special Problems in Budgeting — 103

9.1	Advanced manufacturing technology (AMT)	103
9.2	New products	103
9.3	Main areas of advanced manufacturing technology	104
9.4	Computer-aided design (CAD) and computer-aided manufacture (CAM)	104
9.5	Flexible manufacturing systems (FMS)	104
9.6	Computer-integrated manufacture (CIM)	105
9.7	CIM and budgeting	105
9.8	World class manufacturing (WCM)	105
9.9	Total quality control (TQC)	105
9.10	Just-in-Time (JIT) manufacturing	106
9.11	JIT production method	106
9.12	Characteristics of JIT	106
9.13	JIT materials budgeting	107
9.14	JIT materials control	107
9.15	JIT control of payables	107
9.16	JIT labour budgeting	107
9.17	JIT total budget	108
9.18	JIT standard times	108
9.19	JIT labour budgeting and control	108
9.20	JIT labour control reports	109
9.21	JIT overhead budgets	109
9.22	JIT overhead recovery and control	109
9.23	Irrelevance of traditional management accounting	110
9.24	Performance measures and control for world class manufacturing (WCM)	110
9.25	Incremental budgeting	111
9.26	Zero-base budgeting (ZBB)	111
9.27	Advantages of ZBB	112
9.28	Cost management process (CMP)	112
9.29	Outcome of ZBB and CMP	114
9.30	Issues raised under ZBB and CMP	114
9.31	Performance monitoring under ZBB and CMP	115

9.32 Additional resources under ZBB and CMP   115
9.33 Advantages of CMP   115
9.34 Disadvantages of ZBB and CMP   115

10 *Examples of Company Budgeting Procedures*   117

A regional newspaper group   117
10.1   Budgeting   117
10.2   Organisation structure   117
10.3   Timetable and tasks in preparing group budgets   117
10.4   Performance monitoring and control   119
10.5   Key financial factors   119
10.6   Key business issues   120

A retail supermarket chain   121
10.7   Budgeting   121
10.8   Relation of forecasts to budget   121
10.9   Relationship of budget to long-term plans   121
10.10 Bottom up and top down approaches   121
10.11 Budget guidelines   121
10.12 Financial statements   122
10.13 Budget timetable and sequence of events   122
10.14 Key issues   123

A retail fashion chain   124
10.15 Budgeting   124
10.16 Budget period and financial year   124
10.17 Planning process   124
10.18 Five-year plan   124
10.19 Full year plans   125
10.20 First half plans   125
10.21 Second half plan   126
10.22 Monthly performance monitoring   126
10.23 Area performance review   127
10.24 Regional performance review   127
10.25 Finance review   127
10.26 Central cost review   128
10.27 Preparation of monthly finance package   128
10.28 Preparation of board papers   128
10.29 Key elements in the budget   129
10.30 Monitoring retailing   130

An aerospace and defence systems company   130
10.31 Budget management   130
10.32 Budget timetable   130
10.33 Tasks and deadlines   130
10.34 Personnel and cost trends   131

10.35	Sales forecasts	131
10.36	Sales budget and stock levels	131
10.37	Materials and labour requirements	131
10.38	Development and general engineering	131
10.39	Factory operating budget	131
10.40	Trading budget	132
10.41	Funds budget	132
10.42	Tax, interest and cash flow	132
10.43	Key budget statistics	133
10.44	Headcount	133
10.45	Key budget indicators	133
10.46	Budget comparisons	134
10.47	Standard cost up-date	134

An international food and drinks group — 135

10.48	An example of published company objectives	135
10.49	Business objectives	135
10.50	Financial objectives	135

11 Specimen Forms

137

11.1	Profit and loss account.	137
11.2	Phased (quarterly) profit and loss account	137
11.3	Balance sheet	137
11.4	Phased (monthly) balance sheet	137
11.5	Funds flow statement	137
11.6	Phased (monthly) funds flow statement	138
11.7	Phased (monthly) cash and funds flow statement	138
11.8	Capital expenditure summary	138
11.9	Phased (monthly) capital expenditure summary	138
11.10	Brand profitability analysis	138
11.11	Discretionary marketing expenditure	138
11.12	Brand price analysis	138
11.13	Other income and expenditure and exceptional items	139
11.14	Estimated tax computation	139
11.15	Phased current liabilities	139
11.16	Newspaper product prices	139
11.17	Newspaper revenue and cost variance analysis	139
11.18	Wages, materials and expenses variance	139
11.19	Phased (monthly) employee and payroll costs	139
11.20	Cost allocation analysis	139
11.21	Branch and head office controllable expenses	140
11.22	Phased (monthly) stocks analysis	140
11.23	Analysis of debtors	140
11.24	Key costs and productivity ratios	140
11.25	Downside sensitivity analysis	140

11.26 Transfer price analysis   140
11.27 Profit and loss control statement   140
11.28 Variance summary explanations and actions   141
11.29 Forecast variance summary   141
11.30 Market share analysis   141
11.31 Net debt analysis   141

Forms   143

Bibliography   175

Index   177

Acknowledgements

The first steps to producing this guide were taken in 1985 and the Institute thanks the following members of the Working Party who conducted the investigations and carried out the preparatory work: E B Bishop (Chairman), P E A Shailer, A J Bailey, M. Greenwood, T Cook, V Daniel, K Howard, D Allen, G A Wright and B Cox (Secretary of the working party).

The following companies released members for the Working Party, provided materials from company manuals and allowed generous time for interviews: Cadbury Schweppes Ltd, Wimpey PLC , J Sainsbury Ltd, Thompson Regional Newspapers Ltd, Top Shop Ltd and Guinness Breweries PLC.

The Institute also thanks Professor D Garbutt PhD MEd FCMA ACIS AcDipEd, who conducted extensive further research and wrote the guide.

Abstract

Making Budgets Work – has been prepared as a practical guide to the use of budgets in business organisations based on current expertise and experience of professional management accountants.

The guide aims to help *management accountants* to:

- apply financial disciplines to the management of organisations;
- set up and operate a budgetary control system.

The guide will also assist

'non-financial' managers and *small-business executives:*

to obtain insight into the positive contribution which budgeting can make to planning and controlling their organisation.

The guide summarises current concepts and practice and provides a check list of the main considerations involved in budgetary control. As far as possible, terminology used in the guide follows the definitions in the revised *'CIMA Terminology'*. Example forms and procedures also show how co-operating companies use budgeting in the management of their organisations

There is an underlying logic common to all the systems used by the companies but their procedures and practices reflect needs which differ according to the type of products they make and the markets into which they sell.

The technological character of the products and services offered by companies is changing rapidly and this, also, affects the kind of information system they require.

The size of the enterprise influences the patterns of communication which is built into the organisation and budgetary control system, and the organisational and management styles are naturally reflected in the style of budgeting adopted.

This guide is intended to be a useful practical aid to management accountants, executives and managers and every effort has been made to keep it up-to-date and reliable. The examples are realistic but not a ready made set of prescriptions. The user will be able to use the guide as a source of ideas, but will have to adapt these to his or her own circumstances.

Budgets are essentially a management tool and 'non-financial managers' from marketing, production and services may use the guide as an introduction to the common core of concepts and procedures which underpin budgetary control systems.

This guide was drawn up largely on the basis of company instruction manuals, but where gaps occurred, these were filled through personal interviews with senior management accountants in the co-operating companies.

Each chapter commences with a statement of some key questions addressed in the chapter. In answering these questions, the guide incorporates advice, based on the experience of major companies, on how these questions are answered in practice.

The guide starts by defining some key terms and then looks at the crucial decisions on scope, objectives, decision needs and responsibilities needed to get budgetary control under way.

For effective budgeting, the organisation must determine who will lead the organisation of budgeting and what committee and administrative structures and procedures are needed to develop and implement the business objectives. Normally, the Chief Executive will play a leading role to ensure both organisational and financial viability. The management accountant also plays an important role in budgeting because the assessment of financial viability is a constant concern as selling and operating budgets are developed. Many issues require complex and careful analysis and the financial statements of profit, cash flow and balance sheet position must be continually up-dated.

Budgets must be based on a clear strategy. The business compares its present standing to the changing environment and prepares a strategic plan to close the gap between desired and likely results. This leads to the definition of business objectives, from which financial objectives and targets are developed and on which budgets should be based. For budgeting purposes, the key goals will be mainly financial and the adoption of budgets is an important way in which management move towards fulfilment of business and marketing plans. The budgets for revenues and incomes must be firmly based on plans which analyse the product markets and the market share for which the organisation can aim. The marketing policies must establish detailed marketing mix for new and old products and services in the light of product life cycles.

The development of operating and expenditure budgets should be based on a systems approach which identifies the required outputs which will be obtained from each activity, and then determines what input resources should be allocated to achieve the objectives. The budgets need to establish such factors as activity measures, efficiency measures, and headcount as well as costs. It is also important that all assets coming on stream during the budget period be budgeted for, together with the associated costs of maintenance and repair.

Cash flow and working capital budgets measure the funding of the organisation rather than its profitability and must be prepared during all stages of budgetary control and whenever profit and loss accounts and balance sheets are drawn up, although they usually cover a longer interval than the budget period.

Performance monitoring and control are based on comparisons of actual to budgeted results and control points must be identified to which reports are directed. The budgetary control system must be integrated with other management information systems and frequent reports must provide feedback in time for corrective actions to be taken. During the budget period some companies combine the budgets and actuals with forecasts to get a more realistic assessment of performance. Budget review meetings may discuss results and it is important to monitor non-financial as well as financial objectives.

The aims of a budgetary control system are to develop and implement plans, co-ordinate sections and departments, and monitor performance in the light of plans. The system will only work if it is used by managers and supervisors and if it leads to corrective actions.

It has been suggested, notably by *Professor Kaplan*, that management accounting is in a state of crisis. The book reviews the changing production and selling environment of businesses and some of the newer manufacturing strategies such as 'World Class Manufacturing' and 'Just-in-Time' which are widely advocated. Certainly, some of the traditional approaches to budgeting must be abandoned as the organisation fits the system to its current needs.

Chapter 10 incorporates examples of budgetary control systems provided by the companies taking part in the study and Chapter 11 reproduces a number of actual forms.

The book concludes with a bibliography and index.

1
General Considerations: An Introduction to Budgeting

This chapter raises various questions which will be elaborated later in the book, including:

- What is budgeting ?
- What is budgetary control ?
- What is strategic budgeting ?
- What kind of objectives are needed for budgeting ?
- What is performance monitoring ?
- What is the role of the management accountant in budgeting ?

1.1 Budget definition

A budget is a plan of the future activities of an organisation. It is expressed mainly in financial terms but usually incorporates many non-financial, quantitative measures as well.

1.2 Budgetary control

Budgets are the part of the management information system which show the financial implications of the business plans and policies. If budgets are related to the responsibilities of managers and used during the period to compare actual to budgeted results, then budgets are part of the management control system and the firm is using budgetary control.

1.3 Budget statements

A budget takes the form of a set of financial and/or quantitative statements which cover the assumed budget period and include income, expenditure and the employment of capital. The policy to be pursued during the period for the purpose of attaining the objectives is implicit in the budget plan.

1.4 Values, price and quantity

Budgets are stated as a set of money values but generally these values must be calculated from a quantitive element multiplied by a price. The accuracy of the budgets, even if primarily financial, depends as much on the precision of the quantitative measurements as on the prices.

1.5 *Prior preparation and approval*

Budgets should be prepared in advance of the time period for which they are to be used. Surprisingly, this requirement is often ignored.

1.6 *Strategic budgets*

This guide deals with short-term budgeting. Strategic budgets extend five, ten or twenty years ahead and are based on broad strategic objectives. The two must be co-ordinated. For strategic budgeting, see *Simmonds, 1988.*

1.7 *Objectives*

Budgetary control must be based on the setting and achievement of appropriate financial objectives at all levels within an organisation. It is misleading to think in terms of a single objective, even for the simplest budget.

1.8 *Management information*

Budgetary control is a management information system which helps to plan, manage and control an organisation by setting clear quantitative and financial targets and objectives.

1.9 *Performance monitoring and evaluation*

A key element in budgeting is the feedback of information comparing actual to budgeted performance. Performance monitoring shows who is responsible for each element in the budget and gives a sound basis for deciding what actions are necessary to improve the achievement of objectives. The monitoring extends from the Group Board right down to the office, retail outlet or shop floor.

1.10 *Capital expenditure budgeting*

The authorisation of capital expenditure is the subject of an extensive literature and a different set of procedures from short-term budgeting. These are dealt with in CIMA Management Accounting Guide No 6 – Capital Expenditure Control.

1.11 *The role of the management accountant*

The role of the management accountant is to provide financial information, reports, advice and analysis to the many decisions which are made at all management levels.

2
Administration of the Budgetary Process

Among the questions which this chapter seeks to answer are:

- Who should lead the budget process ?
- What fundamentals must be borne in mind when starting to build a budget system ?
- What are the purposes and objectives of budgets ?
- What period should budgets cover ?
- What are continuous and rolling budgets ?
- What factors affect the structure of a budget ?
- Why is it necessary to define the budget objectives ?
- Must budgets be decentralised to obtain involvement of managers ?
- How can the budgeting process be organised ?
- What stages and tasks are involved in preparing draft budgets?
- What budgets are required by groups ?
- How are short term budgets related to strategic plans ?
- How is the timetable set ?
- What should the budget manual contain ?

2.1 *Leadership*

The budget process needs effective leadership which means:

(a) full commitment by the chief executive and the board to the entire procedure;

(b) appointment of a budget officer to be responsible for the procedure: this could be the management accountant or a senior member of staff;

(c) setting up a budget committee to oversee the operation of the system, preferably chaired by a board member, with the budget officer as secretary.

2.2 *Starting to build the budgeting system*

Four key points must be borne in mind when starting to build up a budget system:

(1) *Determine scope.* It is unwise to start too ambitiously. The demand for quick results must be balanced against the need for accuracy and realism. The budget controller should decide which companies or divisions in a group, which departments, products, regions and functional groups will be included. Then, the components and sub-components settled upon for which separate budgets will be required. Deciding the scope determines the organisational level at which data will be collected from other systems and at which budgets and results will be reported.

(2) *Define objectives.* The starting point for budgeting must be the business and financial objectives which will apply in the budget period. The detailed operating objectives will emerge as subsidiary budgets are prepared.

(3) *Consider decision needs.* Budgets are intended for managers who control the disposition of corporate resources and the structure must be designed to produce timely information which relates to managerial decisions. In addition, financial reports must be broadly reconcilable with the standard accounting reports and any other reports required by the group or parent company.

(4) *Assign budgeting responsibilities.* A prime objective of budgetary control is to delegate responsibility for cost control to the persons who actually commit resources and incur expenditure. This clarifies responsibilities, gives the person concerned the authority to spend, and improves managerial accountability by facilitating comparisons so that a more objective assessment of performance can be made.

2.3 Budgeting stages

There are three main stages in operating the budget system:

(1) *Budget setting.* Budgets are set up for agreed responsibility levels, in consultation with the responsible managers. Differences are discussed and reconciled and the Master Budget is then formally approved by top management. The business, financial and operating objectives in the budgets then become the targets at all levels.

(2) *Reports.* Personnel for whom targets have been set are provided with information comparing actual performance to budget. The comparisons should lead to corrective actions and may result in incentive rewards. The time periods of reports are shorter than the budget time periods, to encourage corrective actions. For instance, an annual budget may be broken down into monthly reporting periods, monthly budgets broken down into weekly periods, and so on.

(3) *Budget review.* Budgets may be revised as business conditions change during the period and, in any case, the starting point for the next period budget preparation will be a review of the current budgets.

2.4 Budget purposes

Budgets serve more than one purpose. They are used to:

- allocate resources;
- quantify plans;
- set performance objectives and targets;
- co-ordinate departmental activities;
- communicate management plans and objectives;
- plan and control business performance.

2.5 Budget structure

The general structure of the budgets must reflect the organisation and responsibility levels in the company or group for which the budget is produced.

Despite underlying similarities, no two organisations, and therefore no two master budgets, are identical.

Generalised factors common to all budgets are:

- business, financial and operating objectives;
- organisation structure and personnel policies;
- product and service strategy;
- production, distribution, selling and administrative structure;
- market location and marketing methods;
- roll forward of medium-term plans;
- capital investment requirements;
- product costs;
- direct resources consumed and direct costs;
- pricing policy and structure;
- sales and service delivery;
- overhead costs;
- revenues;
- the key financial statements, profit and loss account, balance sheet, cash and funds flow statements.

2.6 Business strategy, planning and objectives

The management planning and corporate strategy of an organisation is guided by business and financial objectives which are closely related.

2.7 Business objectives

Business objectives are an important determinant of budgets even though they may be only partly quantifiable. The business objectives cover such matters as markets, economic and business conditions, organisation style and personnel policies. A more detailed list is given in Chapter 3.

2.8 Financial objectives

A wide range of financial criteria are incorporated in budgets and used to evaluate actual performance. These may be stated in absolute terms, as ranges or as ratios. They include such factors as profitability, liquidity, and use of assets; a more detailed list is given in Chapter 3. Financial objectives should be reflected in the detailed objectives which are developed for departments, functions and products.

2.9 Operating objectives

Many measures of resource allocation and utilisation can be identified and used in the preparation of budgets. To some extent they relate to the measures of business and financial objectives. Operating objectives must also be directly related to the measurement and comparison of operating activities. The evolution of realistic measures of operating performance is a key activity in short-term budgets and control. These indicators should be incorporated into budgets at the relevant levels. Detailed examples are given in Chapter 5.

2.10 Clear and measurable objectives

The objectives and targets set by the budgets should be both clear and measurable. People must know for what they are being held accountable and what is its ultimate effect on the organisation. For instance, a divisional manager may be responsible for profit because he is responsible both for selling and production or procurement. A sales manager may be responsible for sales performance but not for product cost.

2.11 Key budget factors

The budget should be calculated on factors which clearly relate to the way the organisation operates commercially. The key factors affecting profits and costs should be identified, and particularly the underlying relationships with commercial factors in the business. For example, a firm operating a distribution fleet will budget average miles per trip, average number of trips, standard load and unload times, distribution volumes and marginal business. In process industries, sales volume and gross margin are important measures of performance because of high fixed production costs in the short term. An example is shown as Form 11.24. In jobbing industries, production costs are more controllable and net profit is a better measure.

2.12 Budget centres

Budget centres are areas of control which match budgets and reports to the responsibilities of managers. The organisation has two main dimensions which must be reflected in the budget centres:

(1) *Horizontally across the organisation*
The organisation may be divided into regions and/or product ranges. Sometimes these go together, as when one product is produced only in one region. More often they are separate, for instance when one product is marketed in several or all regions. There may also be cross relationships financially, as is the case when products are transferred from producer to marketing region, or when a UK subsidiary of a US parent takes responsibility for sales to the Commonwealth. Functionally specialised departments may also be organised horizontally, such as when Research and Development or Management Consultancy is a group function.

(2) *Vertically up and down the organisation*
The organisation is normally organised in a hierarchy in which responsibilities are defined from top to bottom. This hierarchy allocates duties which people must perform and responsibilities for which they are held accountable. Reporting on budgeted performance is an important, but not the only, element in managerial accountability.

The fact that the vertical hierarchy is combined with horizontal product, regional and functional divisions creates difficulties in designing the budget system.

2.13 Types of budget centre

The type of budget centre used in an organisation will depend on many factors including the technology in use, the organisation structure and the managerial philosophy. In general, budgets should be related to information needs and discretion in making decisions.

The types of budget centre include:

- *Rate of return centres.* Divisions or companies responsible for revenues, costs and assets employed may be budgeted on a rate of return basis.
- *Profit centres.* Managers responsible for both revenues and costs may be budgeted on a profit centre basis.
- *Cost centres.* Managers and supervisors responsible only for costs may be budgeted on a cost centre basis.

- *Physical factor centres.* The factors to which personnel relate tend to be non-financial at the lower levels of the organisation. For instance a foreman may need information solely on budgeted, standard and actual hours worked/produced, or a salesman on numbers sold.

At the higher levels, where managers are responsible for cost and profit centres, it is likely the budgeting will be more financially orientated so that achievement of business objectives can be monitored and comparisons made across the group.

2.14 Controllable costs and revenues

Budget formats should separate controllable from non-controllable costs and revenues so that budgets reflect the costs, revenues and assets for which people are responsible. Since fixed costs are the result of policy decisions, only the managers responsible for the policies should be held accountable for such costs.

Manufacturing budgets often include allocated costs or charges for services which are correctly required for total product costs, but it is wrong for the manager to be held responsible for the allocated costs over which (s)he has no control. In a retail chain, the branch budgets may include rent or notional rent charged, in order to calculate branch profitability, but the branch manager is not held responsible for that cost since (s)he has no control over it. Nevertheless, as branch results or product and manufacturing costs are consolidated upwards, there is a level at which more senior management is responsible for these costs and, ultimately, all costs. See Form 11.21 for an example.

2.15 Flexible budget comparisons

Budgets for variable costs should be flexed to take account of the volumes of sales and production. During budget preparation, estimated cost data at various levels of production may be used to determine the optimum level. When the budget is implemented, the budget allowances will increase or decrease according to the sales or production levels actually attained.

2.16 Budget period

The time span to which the plan of action relates is commonly one year but may be longer or shorter. The budget period affects both form and content, for example:

- *short-term budgets* (one year or less) emphasise short-term control and operating profitability;

- *medium-term budgets* (one to five years), emphasise the filling of gaps in current corporate strengths and the balance between capital and current spending;
- *long-term budgets* (five years or more) emphasise the development of viable strategies which will secure long-term survival.

These distinctions are not hard and fast, but each type leads to a different budget design. Reconciling the budgets needs careful planning.

2.17 *Natural business year*

It is important to consider the dates on which the budget period should start and end. Most service and product-orientated companies have a definite cycle of activities covering one year and there may be one or more periods when sales peak. Since the activities being co-ordinated, such as producing in anticipation of selling, often fall into different months, it is vital to make sure they do not also fall into different budget periods. Otherwise the benefits of budgeting in planning and co-ordinating may be lost.

2.18 *Seasonal factors*

Many factors in the budget may be subject to seasonal variation which should be identified and used in preparing the budgets and later in reporting. Some factors such as the timing of deliveries or the date of raising invoices for calculating income from sales may be less predictable.

2.19 *Control period*

Short-term budgets normally apply to a one-year period but the budget period is divided into shorter intervals for control purposes, so that action can be taken if actual results diverge from budget.

2.20 *Calendarisation*

Splitting down the budget amounts into shorter intervals is known as calendarisation. The values should be calendarised correctly over the budget period, so that the relevant factors such as weather and vacations are identified and the money allocated accordingly. This means that variances will be reported more accurately when the time comes.

The Forms in Chapter 11 include several examples of monthly phased reports and one based on quarters.

2.21 *Continuous and rolling budgets*

Budgets require regular review and modification to reflect rapidly changing business conditions. In continuous budgeting, budgets are reset on a short cycle, perhaps monthly or quarterly. Rolling budgets cover a period such as a year but are 'rolled forward' monthly by dropping the first month and adding a month at the end.

2.22 *Flexible budgets and accounting policies*

Flexible budgets make it more difficult to comply with some accounting policies such as a requirement that full cost overheads are included in stock valuations and used in calculating trading profits. Reconciliation statements should be prepared to show the adjustments which will have been made during the budget period.

2.23 *Operating budgets*

The overall plan of operations for the business is expressed in an operating budget which is usually prepared in two dimensions:

(1) *Responsibility budgets*
Responsibility budgets put the budget centre costs, incomes and assets in relation to the persons responsible for implementing them. This is a flexible budget for variable costs and incomes. Form 11.21 is an example.

(2) *Programme budgets*
Programme budgets set out the costs, incomes and assets according to the line of action to be taken, e.g. by product or service or customer. Forms 11.10 to 11.12 are examples used in budgeting for brands.

2.24 *Service department budgets*

With progressive automation there is a decrease in production personnel and an increase in service and specialist departments who may not be engaged on current production at all. Such departments account for the growing proportion of fixed overhead costs and will be allocated a fixed budget.

2.25 *Principal budget factor*

This is the main element determining the level of business activity, usually the sales demand but there may also be a limiting factor in production such as material shortages or skilled labour.

2.26 *Master budget*

The master budget is the complete set of budgets, with all the supporting detail, which is finally approved by top management for implementation at the start of the budget period.

2.27 *Centralisation versus decentralisation*

The system may be centralised or decentralised. (See *Arnold, 1987*).

- In a centralised system, control is exercised over cost elements, such as salaries, accommodation, purchasing, etc., across the board.
- In a decentralised system, control is exercised by cost centre, profit centre or profitability centre.

Effective budgetary control uses budgets to control the activities of an organisation. It is often argued that decentralised budgets will foster commitment and understanding because the people involved in the process of producing their own budget are then held responsible for implementation. Centralised budgets prepared by accountants, even management accountants, and then handed out to operating managers will not be acceptable because they do not reflect the real situation and the actual management methods in use. For example, *Arnold, 1987*, cites the legal division of a central Government department which had responsibility for storing all departmental documents. Since it was obliged to store all documents sent to it, it could not control costs. The situation was changed by the introduction of budgetary control and a system for recharging storage costs with a consequent reduction in the number of documents stored. Involving concerned managers at all levels should produce more realistic targets based on consensus and commitment. The authority to spend saves staff time and effort.

In another example, *Arnold, 1987*, quotes an organisation which introduced a budgeting system which, *inter alia*, made local managers responsible for authorising overtime so long as it was within budget. The effect was to give quicker decisions and a saving of time because managers did not have to refer to head office for approval in each case. Managers may also cut costs or improve profitability by changing the mix of resources according to local requirements, for instance by changing the balance between professional and administrative staff.

2.28 *Integrated control systems*

The budgetary control system is only one of many systems through which management directs the organisation and it should be integrated with these other systems. For example:

- *Control of sales and production.* In this aspect of control, managers are using resources to achieve target levels of activity which are intended to attain budgeted profitability targets, or better. Variances should report on the physical inputs and outputs as well as on the associated costs and benefits.
- *Financial accounting controls.* In this aspect, controls are established over expenses and accounting policies, and budgetary control could be asked to

measure the effectiveness of the detailed instructions issued. With accounting policies compliance, it may be necessary to show reconciliations between the valuations used for budgets and those required by the accounting policies.

2.29 *Preparing a draft budget*

The preparation of budgets goes through a number of stages at which drafts are prepared and then amended in the light of discussions between managers, subordinates, departments and functions. The following sequence is typical:

(a) *Timetable*. Prepare and circulate a timetable to involved persons.

(b) *Key factors*. Identify the key commercial factors which will affect the business in the budget period. This involves analysing the potential markets for products, activities of competitors, and planned new product introductions. The whole strategic position of the company should be considered.

(c) *Guidelines*. Prepare, for the managing director or board to circulate to involved managers, a set of guidelines stating the key budget factors and conditions which will apply in the budget period. A tentative statement of financial performance must be included. The key financial ratios should reflect the commercial factors. Some, such as trading profit to turnover are in general use, others will be specific, such as contribution per square foot in retailing, or gross margin for process industries.

(d) *Prepare draft budgets*. Through the budget committee and sub-committees, prepare draft budgets. This will involve expressing the overall guidelines into the factors affecting particular departments such as trends in quantity discounts, debtor days outstanding, shipment delays and so on.

Where at all possible, the drafts will be prepared to conform to the board guidelines, but where, after discussions and analysis, the drafts do not conform to guidelines, explanations should be prepared, along with statements showing the effects that conformity to guidelines would have on commercial performance, costs, revenues and assets employed.

It may be useful to combine the review of current budgets with the preparation of new budgets.

The budget officers should anticipate any problems likely to affect profits and some allowances may have to be made for contingencies such as a downturn in sales after devaluation in a Third World country or a strike over a pay award. Contingency funds are held centrally unless the items are relatively small.

(e) *Draft master budget*. The management accountant should prepare a consolidated draft master budget with accompanying financial statements including the calculation of financial performance and other ratios.

2.30 *Tasks, objectives and information in budget preparation*

The tasks to be accomplished, the information required and the objectives can be summarised as follows:

Tasks	Objectives	Information Needed
1 Analysing strategic issues	Guidelines for detailed forecasts and plans	Relevant sections of corporate plan and divisional plans
2 Quantification in detail of functional, departmental or organisation plans in terms of money and human resources	Construction of a master budget. (This includes a profit and loss account and balance sheet)	Sales forecasts, production plans, research and development plans, marketing, distribution and publicity plans, selling and administration plans
3 Constructing functional and divisional and master budget: capital expenditure revenue operational expenditure research and development expenditure cash flow	To establish claims for resources required to achieve budget plans	Quantified functional divisional or organisation plans for budget period including: capital expenditure projects
4 Reviewing budgets at senior management level together with budget preparers, comprising: review exercise; communications exercise	To ensure proper relationship with strategic issues. To ensure proper communication and understanding at all levels as to divisional ideas and needs, total resources available	Relevant sections of corporate plan, divisional plans, master budgets, appraisal reports concerning master budget, notes of budget meetings
5 Structuring overall or final master budget and subsidiary budgets	Formalising the control parameters for the budget year i.e. 'setting the budgets'	Approved head office and divisional master budgets

2.31 *Setting the budget timetable*

The management accountant or budget officer will set a financial calendar describing the budget process over the budget period. This should show how the budgeting work fits in with other financial work and deadlines. The calendar should indicate clearly the key dates at which progress towards completion can be assessed. The budget process involves managers throughout the organisation and they will also have their own key events and timetables which may be commercially more important than the budgeting deadlines, e.g. the build up to the peak Christmas selling period. If the budget timetable is to work it must be related realistically to these departmental timetables which reflect the natural budget year.

Budget preparation should not conflict with financial deadlines, for instance, the start of budgeting might interfere with preparation of interim results and the completion time with end of year accounts. Budget preparation takes time and sufficient allowance must be made for consultation, negotiation, and recalculations. It is common for the resulting budget cycle to extend over three to six months.

2.32 *Completion time*

Agreement and implementation of the budget must be completed just prior to the start of the new budget period, normally the next financial year.

2.33 *Starting time*

The budgeting starting time should be worked out backwards from the completion date allowing sufficient time for completion of the preparatory work. Commencing about the time that first half year results are available should ensure that the preliminary guidelines are firmly based on factual information.

2.34 *Budgets required by group or parent companies*

The budgets required will depend on the management philosophy and organisational structure of the parent. At one extreme, the group may control the component companies or divisions purely on return on investment. In this case, so long as the subsidiary produces a satisfactory return, the parent will require no more than reliable financial accounts submitted monthly, quarterly or even half-yearly.

At the other extreme, some parents run their subsidiaries similar to departments. In this case, the subsidiaries may prepare or be given only cost or sales budgets and a full analysis of variances, sometimes in great detail, may be required monthly plus *ad hoc* reports to answer specific enquiries. Nevertheless, at some point in the chain of control a full set of budgets will be required.

2.35 *Group/parent objectives*

The objectives of a group will be set within the context of a group strategic plan and group managers will make investment decisions within the context of achieving strategic objectives. There will be a greater emphasis on the effect of short-term performance, and therefore short-term budgets, than on longer term plans and budgets. Some companies within a group may find themselves regarded by the group as growth or as declining businesses. Growth businesses will attract support and further investment, declining businesses will not, even though they may be more profitable ! These attitudes will affect capital investment, access to new markets and manning levels.

2.36 *Market trends and competition*

The group is likely to be strongly influenced by stock market trends and by the activities of competitors. These may translate into internal targets such as earnings per share which then must be worked back into operating profits before tax, trading margins, sales turnover and cash flow targets.

2.37 *Relation to strategic plans*

Since parent companies are monitoring the long-term strategic development of the group, they are likely to require three to five year plans from subsidiary companies. The plans may require the use of financial models of future profit and loss accounts, balance sheets and funds flow statements linked to the variables for each major subsidiary. There may be no more than half a dozen factors such as sales volumes, prices, contribution or profit per employee, operating profit related to fixed assets employed, or profit per relevant input unit. Since these strategic plans determine investment decisions, it is advisable to ensure that the short-term budgets and plan are consistent with them.

2.38 *Budgets for subsidiaries*

The starting point for the subsidiary's budgeting must be the group plans and defined strategy and the criteria on which the group will judge the performance of subsidiaries. The objectives of subsidiaries should be clearly related to those of the group or parent company. The scope of the subsidiaries budgets depends on the extent to which their managements are held accountable for them. It follows that the budgets constructed by subsidiaries can be constructed in terms which reflect the nature of their own business so long as they ultimately incorporate group criteria on performance. The group will require the return of a limited number of key forms reporting on the criteria important to them, and the subsidiary should ensure that these can be completed as a routine from an edited version of the subsidiary budgets and performance reports. The development of two systems should be avoided.

2.39 *Tax planning and treasury function*

A clear decision should be taken on whether the group will have centralised tax planning and treasury functions. These functions are usually centralised in order to maximise returns on group investment, but the consequence is that local management will have no control over cash and taxation. Some group decisions may not be understood by local managers. Form 11.14 shows an example of the computations required for tax planning in the budgeting process.

2.40 *Budget timetable for a group*

A group composed of a number of subsidiaries sets the following timetable:

(a) *Guideline budgets.* Six months before the year end, outline budgets for the next three to five years for the group are prepared, taking account of current year's performance and achievement of strategic objectives. This gives the guidelines within which budgets and targets are determined. Not all subsidiary companies and departments are given targets at this stage, but if not, they receive an indication of the performance parameters which are be expected to be applied for the next year. A limited number of input and output factors are identified and quantified and the tentative departmental budgets are compared and adjusted to give a 'fair' balance.

(b) *Draft budgets.* Subsidiaries prepare their budgets to conform with the outline targets or parameters. The companies are also expected to ensure that expectations of efficiency improvements have been achieved by each department involved. If the parameters are faithfully followed, all subsidiary budgets should be consistent and proper targets and standards will have been set.

(c) *Head office review.* The group head office reviews all budgets for conformity with long-term plans. The review checks that:

- group expenditure is within cash flow limits;
- the balance between each subsidiary ensures that sales volumes are up to required levels;
- the group can meet its targets;
- where necessary, provisional amended targets and parameters are worked out.

(d) *Revised drafts.* Budgets are reviewed with the subsidiaries using the new targets and parameters and the subsidiaries then go back to redraft their budgets in consultation with their own departments.

(e) *Final budgets.* New budgets are submitted by the subsidiaries and reviewed by group head office until a final agreement is reached from all subsidiaries to commit themselves to implementation and achievement of the revised budgets.

(f) *Profit protection plans.* At this stage, profit protection plans are devised to offset events during the budget year which are uncertain in their effects and/or timing but which would make the budgets unrealistic and very difficult to achieve if they actually occurred. The profit protection plans may provide for various measures such as:

- cost cutting to offset the effects of a down-turn in sales volume;
- bringing forward the introduction of new products to meet inadequate sales volumes.
- deferring capital expenditure to restrain cost rises or defer capacity increases.

  These plans are prepared by head office but the plans are discussed with subsidiaries likely to be affected by them. All these measures may also have long term implications which are considered in the light of the strategic plans. See Chapter 10 for some further examples.

2.41 *Developing the budget manual*

The budget manual should be developed by the budget officer and his staff in consultation with all staff involved in budget preparation and reporting.

2.42 *Contents of the budget manual*

The budget manual is a complete description of the budget process setting out rules and procedures for the whole process of budgetary control.

The manual should be split into sections, for instance:

(a) a general introduction to the budgeting process in the organisation and the objectives in setting up the system;

(b) importance of the budgeting process to the organisation;

(c) an overview of the budgeting timetable;

(d) the budget timetable for the current year with dates and deadlines;

(e) the company organisation and the matching structure of the budgets;

(f) the budget committee structure;

(g) duties and responsibilities of the committees, budget director, departmental heads, and others responsible for the preparation and administration of budgets;

(h) how and why budget guidelines are prepared;

(i) the guidelines for the current year;

(j) how to prepare budgets in each section of the organisation and in accordance with guidelines e.g.

- marketing;
- production;
- functional departments such as research and development, public relations;
- service departments such as administration and accounting;

Departments may only receive the section of the manual which relates to them.

(k) a complete list of forms:
- why each form is needed;
- how to complete each form;

(l) an explanation of the control process, e.g.
- what are variances ?
- what uses can be made of variance analysis;
- how can the budgeting staff help;

(m) a statement of the control information which:
- will be supplied routinely and how frequently;
- is available on special request and how to obtain it;

(n) technical guidance for the management accountant and his staff on the treatment of various items and the manner in which various forms need to be completed and processed.

(o) a list comprising the budget officer and his staff showing who should be contacted for specific problems.

2.43 *Classification and coding of accounts*

The management accountant must establish a comprehensive and consistent system for classifying and coding accounts which firmly links the management accounts to the budget and control documentation.

3
Financial Objectives and Budgets

This chapter looks at questions which include:

- Why are clear financial objectives needed in budgeting ?
- What should the financial budgets contain ?
- What different planning levels can be identified ?
- How important are the marketing plans ?
- What factors influence business objectives ?
- In what ways may objectives be expressed ?
- What measures apply to the Profit and Loss Account and the Balance Sheet ?
- Who sets the objectives ?
- How can budget guidelines be prepared ?
- Why are standard definitions needed ?

3.1 *The key role of financial objectives in budgeting*

Other objectives may be more important to business success but clear financial objectives are key indicators of business achievement and essential to effective budget planning. Financial objectives must be:

(a) set in the guidelines issued at the start of the budgeting process;

(b) incorporated in the summary or master budget where the profit and loss accounts and balance sheets show the financial objectives to be achieved in the budget period;

(c) worked through systematically into the budgets for income, expenses, liabilities and asset deployment which are prepared in detail during the budgeting process; *and*

(d) monitored throughout the budget period, in detail, at all budget levels, so that management can show how the financial objectives are in fact being achieved.

3.2 *The financial budgets*

The financial budgets normally comprise:

- profit and loss account;
- cash flow and working capital statements.

This chapter concentrates on the profit and loss account and balance sheet. Cash flow and working capital statements are dealt with mainly in Chapter 7. Examples of suitable forms are given in Chapter 11.

3.3 Contents of financial budgets

The profit and loss account, balance sheet and cash flow forecasts must contain all the significant elements of income, expenses, operating expenditure, liabilities and asset uses which determine whether the financial objectives will be achieved. For instance, if the key financial objective is to achieve earnings of 100p per share, then the earnings figure will come from the profit and loss account and the number of shares during the budget period from the balance sheet. To establish responsibilities for income and expenses, the budgeted profit and loss account must show the various main sources of revenue, less the matching expenses charged against them. The balance sheet will disclose the shareholders' equity, assets employed and liabilities, and again it must be clear where the responsibility for these items lies.

3.4 Two levels of financial planning

Financial planning may take place at two distinct levels with somewhat different but related objectives.

(1) *At the corporate level,* planning is orientated towards long-term strategic aims intended to secure a profitable future for a large enterprise by the allocation of resources among different business units and markets. The corporate headquarters will monitor the key financial ratios achieved by subsidiaries such as return on capital employed, and will provide guideline objectives which they expect subsidiaries to achieve.

(2) *At the business level,* planning is orientated towards tactical actions and targets designed to secure the survival of a particular business. Business objectives are based on key commercial factors which are used to measure the competitive position of the business unit, within the objectives and constraints set by corporate objectives. The financial objectives, including profitability, are the starting point for budgeting for the business unit which is normally far more detailed than at the corporate level.

3.5 Importance of marketing plans

Marketing plans formulate targets and actions in specific product markets which will achieve the corporate and business goals and objectives. From a business viewpoint, the marketing plan is the starting point for business planning, but the plan must be directed towards clear financial objectives, so in this sense financial objectives are the starting point. When adopted, the marketing plan will be implemented by various specific business functions, such as marketing, production, and management accounting. The role of marketing plans in budgeting for income is discussed in Chapter 4.

3.6 *Deciding business objectives*

Business objectives consider the business as a whole and may be only partly quantifiable. Some objectives are quite general, others are more marketing, organisational or financial in nature. See Chapter 10, paragraphs 10.48 and 10.49 for an example of published company and business objectives. The business objectives need to be re-clarified from time to time and especially at the start of the budgeting process. The organisation changes, as does its environment and it is easy to lose sight of fundamental questions such as:

- What rate of return do our shareholders look for ?
- What changes are taking place in our competitors and our markets ?
- How can our business best produce and deliver the products and services which our customers are looking for?

3.7 *Influences on business objectives*

No two firms will set the same objectives because what they want to achieve in a forthcoming budget period will be influenced by:

- the history and current preferences of the business;
- its skills and know-how; *and*
- the resources it can command.

3.8 *Examples of business objectives*

Some examples of business objectives are:

(a) *General*

(i) diversify into new markets and products to reduce the risk attendent on too great a reliance on a limited range of products;
(ii) concentrate on areas of expertise;
(iii) rationalise product streams and sourcing on a global basis;

(b) *Marketing*

(i) achieve 10 per cent growth in sales;

(ii) improve market share from 15 per cent to 18 per cent;

(iii) widen the product range;

(iv) move into new markets and locations.

(c) Financial

(i) increase operating profits to 20 per cent on sales;

(ii) increase return on investment to 12 per cent.

(iii) maximise use of existing assets, reducing invested funds to £4 billion;

(iv) reduce debt equity ratio to 35 per cent.

(d) Organisational

(i) decentralise/centralise;

(ii) review managerial responsibilities and accountability;

(iii) review personnel performance assessment and reward policies;

(iv) introduce more democratic management style.

The organisation must make decisions on the alternatives available and set the specific marketing and financial targets accordingly. The objectives should be stated precisely, and, where suitable, in quantitative terms. See Chapter 10, paragraphs 10.48 to 10.50 for an example of published company objectives.

3.9 Financial budget objectives

The budget objectives should be the financial criteria used to judge the performance of the company. These can normally be calculated from the profit and loss accounts and balance sheet information. Some examples are given below.

(a) Profitability

(i) *Earnings per share* e.g. the company will earn 25p per share in the upcoming budget period, compared to 20p per share in the current year;

(ii) *Return on total assets* e.g. the company will earn 15 per cent on total assets employed, compared to 14 per cent in the current year;

(iii) *Dividend and interest cover* e.g. the company earnings will be sufficient to cover dividends at least twice and not more than four times in the budget period. The current cover is 2.8 times. The profit before interest and tax will cover interest payments at least three times. The current cover is five times.

(iv) *Before and after tax earnings* e.g. earnings after tax will be £7 million and the expected average tax rate is 30 per cent, giving before tax profits of £10 million.

(v) *Fixed costs* e.g. fixed costs will be contained at £12 million, down from £14 million in the current year.

(vi) *Sales, variable costs and margin on sales* e.g. sales will rise to £100 million in the budget year compared to £85 million in the current year. Variable costs will remain at 78 per cent, i.e. £78 million in the budget year and margins at 22 per cent, giving a budgeted gross margin of £22 million.

(b) Liquidity

(i) *Payment and collection periods* e.g. payment will average 36.5 days, giving creditors of £6 million (on trade purchases of £60 million), and collections 45.5 days, giving debtors of £12.5 million (on sales of £100 million).

(ii) *Stock ratio* e.g. stocks will average 36.5 days or £10 million on sales of £100 million.

(iii) *Debt/Equity ratios* e.g. the company will maintain debt of at least 30 per cent of equity but not more than 50 per cent. On an equity of £200 million, this means borrowings will be at least £60 million and not more than £100 million.

(c) Activity

(i) *Asset turnover rate* e.g. the rate will not fall below the current rate of 0.3 times per year;

(ii) *Sales per day* e.g. sales will rise from £233,000 per day tp £274,000 per day.

3.10 Ways of expressing objectives

The objectives must be expressed in terms that make sense for each objective. For example, they can be stated:

- *in absolute terms*, such as sales to reach £2 billion;
- *in relative terms*, such as sales to increase 10 per cent on current year;
- *as a range*, such as stock to sales to be between 10 per cent and 15 per cent;
- *as a ratio*, such as return on total assets to be 16 per cent;
- *as a maximum*, such as debt equity ratio not to exceed 50 per cent;
- *as a minimum*, such as dividend cover of at least twice.

3.11 Profit and loss account and balance sheet measures

A large number of measures are implicit in the above objectives and must be incorporated in the profit and loss account and balance sheet formats. For example:

- earnings after interest and tax;
- profits after interest but before tax;

- earnings after adjustments for extra-ordinary and exceptional items;
- operating profit on trading;
- sales revenues;
- number of shares on issue;
- value of assets used;
- interest charges;
- level of borrowing;
- rates of interest payable;
- tax rates.

This is not a complete list but the budget officer must make sure that the list *is* complete as budgeting commences.

3.12 Board to set objectives

It will be for the board and the chief executive to identify the financial objectives to be set. The budget officer and managers will then have the responsibility for budgeting to the objectives. However, past budget information can be useful in showing feasible targets.

3.13 Departmental, functional and product objectives

All of the financial objectives should be reflected in the detailed objectives which are developed for departments, functions and products. They are incorporated in the sectional budgets and used to evaluate budget and actual performance. How to do this is dealt with in the following chapters

3.14 Preparing budget guidelines

(a) Budget guidelines should start with a statement of the main factors expected to affect the group and/or business in the coming budget period, for example:

- increased competition against certain products or product groups;
- exchange and financial transfer problems in certain countries/areas of the globe;
- rate(s) of inflation expected to apply;
- the expected fiscal/tax regime;
- interest rates;
- any other significant factors which will influence business performance.

(b) The guidelines should state the performance required from each business unit or factor in profitability, for example:

- for each company, the required earnings per share;
- for each company or profit centre, the required rate of return on assets employed;
- for each profit centre, major market and brand, the expected sales levels in value and volume;
- for the companies in general and for specific sectors of the business, the expected behaviour of major cost factors.

(c) The guidelines should state the timetable for budgeting and show when each major stage in the process will be completed.

3.15 *Pro forma financial statements*

Once the guidelines have been set, they should be used to prepare a pro forma profit and loss account and balance sheet. These should include all the major items, as outlined in paragraphs 3.13 and 3.14 above. The financial ratios can then be calculated, showing:

- the pro forma statements conform to the guidelines;
- the implications of the guidelines for the major components of the statements.

The first pro forma will be a summary profit and loss account, as shown, for example, in Forms 11.1 and 11.2. A pro forma balance sheet will be required, as shown, for example, in Forms 11.3 and 11.4. The pro forma financial statements must be accompanied by statements to cover each subsidiary or significant sector of the business. In effect, these begin to spell out the implications of the guidelines for functional and departmental managements.

3.16 *Need for standard definitions*

Standard definitions of income, expense, asset and liabilities must be established from the start. These definitions will be applied throughout the budgeting process, from the pro formas produced to spell out the guidelines, to the draft budgets, to the final budgets set and finally to the actual results monitored against budget. If definitions change, the players will complain that the goal posts are moving! Having said that, it is a fact that few organisations get all their definitions settled at first try. What happens is that a working definition is first established and this is refined as problems are encountered. In this case it is important that proper records of amendments are made.

3.17 *The profit and loss statements*

The factors included in the profit and loss statements are well established, although details do depend on the particular business. The factors include:

(a) *Sales volumes*

- sales volumes will be expressed in a common unit as far as possible, for instance, a brewing company will define volumes in bulk barrels or hectolitres;
- volumes should be net of returns;
- the product range will be grouped by agreed categories so that summaries are on a consistent basis as between units and over time;
- not all sections of the business will use the same unit, for instance a brewing company may also have leisure activities and food products;
- for some sections of the business it is not feasible to define volume at all and in this case the company may use an index of turnover in terms of the currency of the previous year.

(b) *Sales revenues*

Sales revenues can be defined as the amounts receivable for goods and services supplied, but this definition needs to be clarified to show which items are and are not part of sales revenues.

Items which should be separately accounted for are:

- duties such as VAT, customs and excise duties (see Form 11.12 for an example);
- sales within the group;
- technical service fees and royalties receivable;
- cash discounts;
- sales of by-products and scrap.

Items which are likely to be excluded are:

- sales of fixed assets;
- investment income;
- rents receivable;
- interest receivable.

(c) *Duty and taxes, including VAT*

This may be defined as the net duty payable by profit centres after any drawbacks and refunds have been claimed and on purchases from group or associated companies.

(d) *Variable costs*

The variable costs should be defined as those costs which vary directly with output and/or turnover, but excluding duties. For most companies, this covers:

- raw materials;

- bought-in components;
- an element of distribution costs;
- if by-product and scrap sales are not included above in the sales revenue, the amounts may be taken under this heading, as a credit;
- direct labour may be treated as a variable cost.

Fixed costs are dealt with in the following items (e) to (l).

(e) *Discretionary marketing costs*

This covers all expenditure on:
- advertising, including media space and production;
- promotions to trade and customers;
- sponsorship;
- public relations;
- point of sale materials;

- promotion and give away/ reward items;
- new product development costs;
- market research costs for materials and services.
  See Form 11.11 for an example.

(f) *Manufacturing costs*

This should cover all costs, including direct labour, if they are not treated above as variable costs. The manufacturing activities should be defined and may include:
- making and finishing products for sale;
- packaging;
- maintaining inventories of raw materials and finished goods.
  See Form 11.22 for an example.

(g) *Maintenance or engineering costs*

These should be defined and may cover the costs of maintaining:
- manufacturing plant;
- manufacturing buildings;
- office equipment;
- office buildings;
- computers;
- transport.

If not shown here, these items must be identified and included under other headings.

(h) *Distribution costs*

The distribution costs are incurred in transporting finished goods to customers and may include:

- depreciation of the transport fleet;
- vehicle maintenance (if not shown above in (g)
- employment costs of distribution department;
- administration of the distribution department.

(i) *Marketing fixed costs*

These include marketing costs not shown elsewhere such as:

- employment of marketing staff;
- administration of marketing staff;
- depreciation related to the marketing departments.

(j) *Sales force costs*

The costs of the sales force include:

- employment costs of selling and service staffs;
- travelling expenses;
- sales training;
- administration of the sales force.

Where the basic activity is a sales force responsibility, the costs may include:

- maintenance of customer equipment;
- bad debts (sales force responsible for credit control).

(k) *General administration*

This may cover a range of departments such as:

- purchasing;
- personnel;
- legal;
- company secretarial;
- catering;
- finance;
- general site services;
- insurance;
- training;

- it is assumed that research and development are separately accounted for and not allocated to sales budgets.

   The costs include:

- employment costs;
- equipment;
- computers;
- accommodation;
- services such as telephone, fax, data bases, etc.

(l) *Other income/costs*

There should be a category for residual items of cost/income which are not regular or large enough to justify a separate category. Examples are:

- the disposal of fixed assets;
- exchange gains and losses;
- interest costs or income. Form 11.13 is an example.

(m) *Profits*

The various definitions of profit should relate to the appropriate stages at which each appears in the pro forma, for instance:

- after revenues less selling costs, sales margin;
- after sales margin less variable costs, gross margin;
- after gross margin less manufacturing fixed cost, margin on manufacturing;
- after margin on manufacturing less other fixed costs, net profit on operations;
- after profit on operations less interest, profit after interest but before tax;
- after profit after interest less tax, net earnings to shareholders.

3.18 *The balance sheet*

As with the the profit and loss statements, the factors to be included in the balance sheet are well established, although details depend on the particular business. The factors include:

(A) *Fixed assets*

(a) *Goodwill*

This category may remain firmly under group or head office control but must be provided for in the balance sheet format.

(b) Tangible fixed assets

A number of key statements need to be made about the valuation of tangible assets, including:

- what items are to be included, such as plant, equipment, buildings, etc;
- the treatment of leased assets, for example, assets obtained under financial leases should be capitalised if material;
- any exceptions on inclusion/exclusion, for instance buildings may generally be depreciated except for certain types such as hotels and health spas;
- any conditions which apply to certain inclusions/exclusions, e.g. group approval may be needed not to depreciate buildings or to include capitalised leases as assets;
- whether goodwill on the acquisition of businesses may be included;
- whether the cost of investments in associated companies and the share of retained earnings should be stated;
- what is the basis of valuation, such as acquisition cost less depreciation;
- assets on which depreciation is to be allowed or not e.g. land will not be depreciated;
- the rate(s) of depreciation to be used, such as 20 per cent on vehicles;
- methods of depreciation, i.e. whether straight line or reducing balance.
- in what circumstances revaluations are allowed and how they are to be shown;

(c) Trade investments

Long-term investments in companies outside the group, excluding investments in associates (shown above) and the method of valuation. The use of cost valuations for budgeting purposes would not prevent valuation on some other basis for financial reporting purposes.

(d) Investments in subsidiaries

The method of valuation must be defined, e.g at cost at time of acquisition less goodwill written off and excluding any share of post-acquisition reserves.

(e) Investments in associates

Again, the method of valuation will be defined, e.g. cost at time of acquisition less goodwill written off plus group share of post acquisition reserves retained by the associate.

(B) Current assets

(a) Stocks

All material forms of inventories should be listed including:

- purchased goods;
- raw materials;
- work in progress;
- finished products.

The method of valuation should be stated, e.g. at lower of cost or net realisable value, item by item or by groups.

Manufacturing companies must define whether cost includes some or all of:

- raw materials;
- duties where applicable;
- direct labour and expenses;
- the appropriate proportion of production and other overhead.

Wholesaling and retailing operations may define cost as the invoiced cost of goods purchased for resale.

(b) Debtors

Debtors should be separated between external and intra-group debtors. A provision for bad debts may be made on external debtors but not on group debtors. It may also be desirable to separate trade from non-trade debtors.

(c) Cash and deposits

Various categories should be established if the amounts are material. These may include:

- bank current and deposit accounts;
- bank overdrafts and loans;
- government securities realisable within one year and not held for long-term investment purposes;
- building societies;
- short-term deposits with other companies in the group or to associates.

In general amounts should not be netted off, e.g. overdrafts against deposit account balances unless the bank has the right of set-off. The definitions need careful drafting to match the realities of the group situation. For instance, where a group includes a bank as well as trading companies.

(C) Current liabilities

External creditors should be separated from internal or group creditors.

(a) External trade creditors

This may include:

- all creditors and accounts payable within one year;
- payments by customers in advance;
- expense accruals;
- VAT and duties;
- trade bills payable;
- income taxes deducted from salaries.

(b) Group or internal creditors

This includes all trade and non-trade balances due to other group companies.

(c) Overdrafts and short-term borrowings

This includes:

- balances with banks;
- balances with group companies repayable within one year;
- the elements of term loans falling due for repayment within the budget year;

Where a company has lent money short-term to another company within the group, the amount may be shown as a negative internal overdraft. This will facilitate netting off during consolidation.

(d) Current taxation

This represents the taxation:

- on company profits and ACT on dividends payable within the budget year; *and*
- the intra-group element of tax liabilities.

It does NOT include:

- sales taxes such as VAT;
- duty and taxes deducted from salaries.

(e) Dividends

The total of dividends payable within the budget year to all shareholders, including external and group shareholders. The budgeted amount must take account of any proposed:

- new share issues;
- share purchases and redemptions;
- conversions of preference shares and debentures.

(f) Provisions

All non-trading provisions should be included and a breakdown may be required as an attached schedule if the amounts or changes are material.

(D) *Long-term financing needs*

As budgeting proceeds, it is likely that a need for additional long-term financing will appear. The item will be the residue remaining after calculating assets, and subtracting current liabilities and existing long-term liabilities. At the start of budgeting, when guidelines are being prepared, the figures for existing long-term financing (long-term liabilities and owners' equity) can be picked up from the annual accounting returns. The residual amounts may provisionally be recorded under this heading.

It is possible that some of the need may be eliminated by fine tuning the working capital requirements but if a residue still remains, then decisions on long-term financing must be made.

As the decisions on whether to issue debentures or equity are made, the amounts involved are transferred to the appropriate sub-headings, such as:

- issue of new debentures;
- issue of ordinary shares;
- issue of preference shares.

Decisions on long-term financing will be taken partly on internal factors and should be within the guidelines laid down for the:

- ratio of debt to equity;
- required earnings per share;
- target interest cover;
- target dividends;
- target dividend cover.

The methods of long-term financing used also depend on external factors such as:

- market conditions;
- takeover prospects;
- interest rates.

(E) *Liabilities*

A long-term liability is any borrowing which is repayable more than twelve months after the beginning of the budget year or reporting date. Any element of the long-term liability falling due for repayment in the budget period will appear as a current liability (see Current liabilities above).

(a) *Debentures*

Long-term borrowing by means of a formal debenture issue. It will be necessary to distinguish between issues which may differ in respect of:

- maturity date;
- interest terms;
- security backing;
- trustees.

(b) *Finance leases*

The amounts expected to be outstanding on finance leases should be shown.

(c) *Deferred taxes*

The amounts will probably be obtainable from the annual accounting returns and are unlikely to change during the budget period.

(d) *Group loans*

This is the net amount of loans due from and to group companies. It may also function as the statement of the residual long-term financing needs in subsidiary companies which do not have the power to issue long-term financing. In such cases, this category is ultimately part of the capital structure of the group and functions in lieu of additional share capital in the subsidiary. Decisions on long-term financing still need to be made but are made at the higher, group, level (see Long-term financing needs (D) above).

4
Preparing Income Budgets

This chapter considers, among others, the following questions:

- Why do sales budgets have priority ?
- On what information should income budgets be based ?
- How are income budgets related to the strategic budget ?
- What is in a sales plan ?
- How do you arrive at marketing targets ?
- How are income budgets related to the financial objectives ?
- How do you calculate sales and product sales targets ?
- How do you calculate volumes and prices ?
- How can new product viability be judged ?
- How can market supply and demand be analysed ?
- What is the relevance of market mix and market segmentation ?

4.1 *Priority of sales budgets*

For a commercial organisation the sales or income budget is usually the first to be drafted, evaluated and agreed in the course of budget preparation. The reason is that sales achievement determines the practicability of all other budgets. If you can't sell, you are not in business.

4.2 *Basis of the income budgets*

The analysis required to substantiate income budgets can be summarised as follows:

(a) define the markets for the company's product(s);

(b) analyse the demand characteristics of the market(s) for the product(s);

(c) analyse the supply characteristics of the product markets;

(d) determine the market shares which the company can reasonably expect to obtain for each product or product group;

(e) prepare the income or sales budget from volumes and prices predicted on the basis of the foregoing analyses.

4.3 *Relation to strategic income budget*

The starting point for the short-term budget may be the estimates of markets, market shares and income produced as part of the company's strategic planning process, but the plan for the coming budget period will require far more detailed analysis as the strategy figures are updated in the light of new information becoming available.

In some product areas, the short-term budget may plan for higher targets than were envisaged in the strategy plan. In others, progress may be slower. Some product markets may be affected by new factors, such as innovations in technology which require re-tooling or new product developments.

4.4 *The sales plan*

The sales or income budgets are normally based on a sales plan. Income budgeting starts in one large group when head office requires subsidiaries to make a comprehensive review of sales strategies which must address the key tasks and actions provided by the group at the start of the budgeting process.

The plans are divided into three sections:

(1) *The plan to achieve business and marketing objectives.*

This plan makes clear how the sales plan will meet the set business and marketing objectives. It highlights key objectives by brand and discusses the relative weight of attention to be given to new versus existing brands.

(2) *The trade plan*

This plan identifies the key tasks and plans for handling all customers and competitors. Specific attention is given to:

- key account plans;
- prices, margins and discounting plans;
- trade promotional objectives;
- quality control and servicing objectives;
- relationships with retail outlets;
- plans for meeting competition.

(3) *The organisational plan*

This section deals with any planned organisational changes with accompanying cost benefits/penalties, training plans and the implementation of operational standards for the sales force.

4.5 *Marketing targets*

Marketing targets are evolved by:

(a) *analysing market opportunities*

The range of existing products is analysed from various points of view. For instance, if the business sells a particular product to only one age group, the planners may well ask if a similar product can be made to appeal to a different age group or whether a new product can be developed to increase sales to both.

(b) *developing product strategies*

Various strategies in pricing, promotion and targeting are possible. The most profitable will be chosen.

(c) *setting product targets*

The targets will reflect the state of competition and the strategy being followed for each product and product group.

(d) *developing a detailed marketing plan*

The plan will show the tactical implications of implementing the strategy during the budget period.

(e) *evaluating company strengths, weaknesses and performance.*

All sales and income plans must be based on a realistic appraisal of the company's real strengths and weaknesses. It is unlikely that future performance will be wildly in excess of current levels, although it may always be better.

4.6 *Targets for sales*

The previous chapter stated that financial objectives often take the form of ratios based on the budgeted profit and loss account and balance sheet. Key ratios will be based on various factors, including operating profits, assets employed, returns and margins. For instance, operating profits of £150m are required for a 15 per cent return on £1,000m assets employed and if the operating margin is 10 per cent, then sales revenues must be £1,500m.

4.7 *Product sales targets*

The sales can then be split down into products and product groups as a percentage of target sales, for example, Product A £750m (50 per cent), Product B £450m (30 per cent), Product C £300m (20 per cent).

If sales are to increase significantly overall, the proportions obtained may change between products.

4.8 Target volumes and prices

Considerable effort may be needed to turn the target profit into sensible targets for sales volumes and the prices for each product, depending on the market situation of each product. Forms 11.10 to 11.12 are examples of forms used in developing Brand budgets. Forms 11.16 and 11.17 are used in budgeting newspaper prices and revenue and newsprint costs.

4.9 Cost, asset and profit targets

The effect of the target volumes and prices on other variables will have to be considered. Forms 11.17 and 11.18 show the use of variance analysis, comparing proposed budget to previous or actuals.

The main variables are:

(a) variable operating costs

These may fall with increasing volumes of production, but problems of resources in short supply or falling efficiency could lead to a rise in variable costs.

The 'Brewing' section of Form 11.20 illustrates the calculation of variable production costs of proposed volumes to be manufactured.

(b) fixed operating costs

The spread of fixed costs over increased volumes will lead to a fall in product costs but then there may be a point at which additional capacity is required, leading to a rise in fixed costs. The 'Services' section of Form 11.20 illustrates the allocation of cost of services to proposed volumes to be manufactured.

(c) marketing costs

The costs of marketing products may be affected by income plans because of the need to promote products in various ways.

Form 11.11 is used in budgeting for discretionary marketing expenditure.

(d) value of assets used

If new capacity is required the investment will affect the operating assets as shown in the balance sheet and there will be a knock-on effect on the accounting rate of return on assets employed. Current assets such as stocks and trade debtors will increase, if sales rise, with a corresponding rise in assets employed.

(e) *margins and net profits*

Since margins and net profit are residuals, the effects of relatively small changes in the costs and prices can be quite considerable and must be monitored throughout the process of deciding the income budget. Form 11.10 is used in analysing brand profitability. Form 11.25 is used in 'downside' sensitivity analysis to show the effect on revenues, costs and profits of a downturn in volumes.

4.10 *Funding targets*

The income plans will have an effect on the funds required by the organisation, although funding is outside the purview of those responsible for developing the sales plan. The budget officer must monitor funding by preparing revised financial statements, that is, profit and loss account, balance sheet and cash flow/working capital statements. Example forms are in Chapter 11. Particular items to look for include:

- number of shares on issue;
- need for new borrowing;
- rates of interest payable;
- interest charges;
- debt/equity ratio.

4.11 *Marketing strategy*

An effective marketing strategy is the main vehicle for implementing the overall business strategy. The marketing strategy will be implemented through marketing policies and plans which are designed to achieve the marketing objectives. As noted in 4.1 above the sales plans must also include supporting trade and organisational plans.

4.12 *Defining the market(s) for the company's products*

The marketing policy of the firm must be based on a clear statement of which markets the company is serving. Ideally, this will be known because the sales and marketing departments continuously monitor the performance of products and the markets. The managers involved in preparing the income budgets should be expected to know:

(a) *what goods or services customers are expected to buy;*

for example, a steel producer will produce different grades of steel for the medical profession and the shipbuilding industry;

(b) *how the products will be bought;*

for example, a car exhaust manufacturer may produce a limited range of products but these serve two different markets:

- the original equipment market where the customer is a high volume car producer;
- the replacement market where the customer may be a retail chain or car repair shop or a one stop replacement centre;

(c) *by whom;*

for example, a retail fashion chain may be selling a wide variety of products but only to one market, say the 25 to 40 year old woman in the ABC1 social classes;

(d) *why;*

for example, the company should consider the rationale for the different products and markets as well as the profitability in deciding whether to continue products or not, or to enter or leave certain markets.

4.13 *Market segments*

Customers can be grouped by common characteristics which divide the market into segments, differentiated by:

- *demographic features*
  e.g. age, sex, income;
- *sociological characteristics*
  e.g. social class, life style, personality development;
- *behavioural traits*
  e.g. attitudes, response, uses of product;
- *geographic distribution*
  e.g. nation, state, county and so on;
- *product readiness*
  e.g. awareness, desire, intention to buy;
- *industrial markets*
  e.g. type of user, customer size, technology.

4.14 Marketing policy

Marketing policy may be developed from an audit of the market which reviews Strengths, Weaknesses, Opportunities and Threats (SWOT analysis) in respect of the business, competitive and market environments and the business itself. On this basis, realistic marketing objectives strategies and budgets can be set.

4.15 Differential advantage

The aim of marketing policy is to create a differential advantage, in the face of competition, within target segments of the market. Differential advantage can be obtained by a suitable marketing mix (referred to as the four P's), which must be considered at all stages of marketing.

4.16 The marketing mix

Marketing mix consists of the four 'P's':

(a) Product

- Product management;
- Branding;
- Packaging;
- New product development.

(b) Promotion

- Advertising;
- Merchandising;
- Personal selling;
- Sales promotion;
- Public relations.

(c) Price

- Cost-volume-profit analysis;
- Price differentiation.

(d) Place

- Channels of distribution;
- Physical logistics;
- Customer service.

All these elements of marketing mix must be considered in detail in setting the marketing budget.

A key element for the management accountant is the cost-volume-profit analysis, but many of these factors have financial implications on which the marketing staff may well need to turn to the management accountant for technical analysis and advice.

4.17 Global markets

Improvements in communications and the rapid spread of new technologies, means that there may be a strong globalisation of the market. This is reflected in the international character of many companies and in the easy access which even relatively small producers may have to international markets. The production of microchips in the USA and Japan and the manufacture of personal computers in Taiwan and Hong Kong are examples. Globalisation must be considered at all stages of budgeting because it can affect both the marketing and sourcing of products and components. Differing risks and scenarios between territories must be taken into account, based on research into the market.

4.18 Developing the product range

A product is a tangible physical object or an intangible service which can be offered for use, consumption, or enjoyment, and which satisfies a want or need. The company must develop a coherent product range which reflects customer needs, market segmentation and the strengths and capabilities of the organisation. At the start of budgeting for income the company must decide:

(a) if new products are needed in the range and/or if old products should be withdrawn;

(b) whether it wishes to enter new or withdraw from old existing markets;

(c) whether it is realistic to rely on specific proposals for new products becoming available during the budget period to meet the needs.

4.19 Intangible services

Intangible services are often part of the value of a physical object. For example, a motorcar is a status symbol as well as a means of transport. Services may include, and perhaps combine:

(a) personal services, such as those given by entertainers and hotel staff;

(b) places, such as holiday resorts, conference centres, science parks;

(c) activities, such as sport, training, fund raising;

(d) organisations, such as CIMA, the Reform Club, a political party;

(e) ideas, such as philosophies or religions.

4.20 *New products*

Ideally, major firms keep a stream of new products coming on to the market and the board will want to see that the marketing plan and budget provide for these. New products include original products but may also cover new brands, product improvements and product modifications.

A new product may be designed to:

(a) create an entirely new market;

(b) allow a business to enter an established market;

(c) supplement the product line sold in existing markets;

(d) replace existing products and provide greater value to existing customers;

(e) reposition an existing product in a new market or segment;

(f) lower price, perhaps through lower costs or increased volumes.

Before including a new product in the budget it will be essential to justify its commercial viability first.

4.21 *Product viability*

The commercial viability of a product may be judged on the basis of some or all of the following criteria:

(a) Cash generated by the product must cover launch costs within a stipulated payback period. One company expects this to be achieved in the first year.

(b) The product must meet observed consumer needs.

(c) The product must be suited to the company's manufacturing facilities.

(d) A specific target for achievement of market share should have been evolved during the appraisal of the product before launch.

(e) A target should have been set for achievement of brand position e.g. leadership or number two.

(f) The product must come into profitability within a stipulated time after launch. The financial return will be based on the expected market share and this will determine whether the target is acceptable or not. However, the decision to go ahead may not be entirely driven by expected financial results. Loss makers may be included so that a market may be fully covered. There must be a judgement that the company's strategy calls for representation in a full range of market segments even where this means having loss-making products. One company expects profitability to be achieved within two years, before other companies copy the product.

(g) The product must be able to benefit from and contribute to the company image.

(h) In some companies, distribution must be in the same market sector as existing products.

For a further exposition, see CIMA Management Accounting Guide No. 7 – Planning and Control of New Products.

4.22 Analysis of demand characteristics of market(s) served

The purpose of this analysis is to forecast the underlying growth in the company's product and brand markets. Many industries obtain information from institutions, companies and firms specialising in economic and industry forecasts such as:

● *stockbrokers;*

● *business schools;*
  (for example the London Business School, or the Henley Forecasting Centre)

● *consultants:*
  (for example the Economist Intelligence Unit)

If several forecasts are obtained, they are unlikely to agree entirely and company management must form its own view on the best estimate of future growth given all the information available.

Deriving a forecast product market from the more general economic and industry forecasts is not straightforward. For example, a car exhaust manufacturer may predict the growth in the original equipment market from the expected growth in new car manufacture. Product sales may also be affected by technological factors such as substitution or product developments. For instance, the exhaust manufacturer may make allowances for the trend towards longer life exhausts and for Government intervention on emission controls. Some factors, especially in overseas markets may only be known to local managers who should provide appropriate assessments.

4.23 The supply characteristics of markets served

The purpose of this analysis is to:

(a) determine the likely impact of competitor activity on sales prices;

(b) identify the possible impact of competitor activity on the company's share of the market.

Four steps can be identified in the process:

(1) The first step is to identify all major competitors and determine in broad terms what their strategies are. As well as assessing existing competitors, the company must ascertain whether there are likely to be any new entrants, including new sources of imports or withdrawals, including company failures and plant closures.

(2) The second step is to collect as much information on competitors' strategies as possible from such sources as:

- press reports;
- annual reports and accounts;
- stockbrokers circulars and reports;
- information from field staff such as sales representatives.

(3) The next step is to estimate the likely impact of competitor strategies on the market prices and the effect of these on company pricing and product positioning. For example, competitors dropping their prices may open up the opportunity for the company to maintain or even increase its own sales prices if these can be linked with a superior quality image. More often, a fall in price due to cheap imports may have to be met by corresponding reductions in product price.

(4) Once the likely price behaviour has been determined, using the demand and supply estimates, the company will calculate the resulting total market and the shares to be obtained by all major participants, including the company itself.

4.24 *Volume and market share by sector and brand*

The estimates of sales volumes must be made according to the sectors in which various products are competing. The starting point will be existing markets which may increase or fall. Then the company share of the market will be estimated. Market share may also rise or fall, although not as a simple reflection of the total market. For example, a falling market may be expected to eliminate competitors and lead to a rising market share. Within these overall targets, individual products may give increasing or decreasing sales volumes according to the competition and the stage in the product life cycle.

For example, the current market for Product X and its competitors is 50,000 units and Product X sells 20 per cent of the market, i.e. 10,000 units. The market is expected to fall by 20 per cent in the budget year, to 40,000 units, but Product X will increase its market share to 30 per cent, that is 12,000 units.

4.25 Pricing and sales volumes

Sales volumes and prices go together and should be estimated together. The volume of sales will depend on:

(a) the stage in the life cycle of all products;

(b) the competitive situation;

(c) spending on promotion;

(d) the type of sale expected;

(e) cannibalisation.

These factors are discussed in more detail below.

4.26 Key market indicators

From the analysis of demand and supply described in the preceding two paragraphs, three key figures can be expected to emerge:

(a) the expected increase or decrease in market demand, say $x\%$ and the resulting figure for size of total market;

(b) the expected increase or decrease in sales price for each product, say $y\%$;

(c) the expected market share, say $z\%$ of the total market.

4.27 Estimating sales volumes

If the existing market is taken to be m, then the product sales can be estimated in value terms as follows:

$$\text{Sales estimate } S = \frac{mz(1 + x)(1 + y)}{100}$$

where m = existing market,
  z = market share,
  x = change in market demand,
  y = change in sales price.

It may be objected that the above estimate assumes a passive management. If this is accepted, an allowance may be made for management action, as follows:

$$\text{Sales estimate} = \frac{mz(1 + x)(1 + y)}{100} + q$$

where q = the increase in sales brought about by management action.

The sales estimate for the whole company is then the sum of the estimates for each product.

4.28 *Advertising allocations*

The plans for advertising spending must be developed during the development of the market analysis and the estimation of prices and volumes. Where the company has a range of products and brands, the allocations are made by brand/product but there is a residual category to cover general company advertising. See Form 11.11 for an example.

4.29 *Brand and product leadership*

The immense buying power of major retailers exerts pressure on some suppliers to strive for brand and product leadership because the retailers prefer to stock the brand leader plus one other. However, every company does not need to be the market leader, even if it markets some leading brands.

4.30 *Consumer trends, company expertise and resources*

Plans and estimates should be based on a realistic appraisal of general trends affecting the market and the company's ability to capture a share of the market. Even if a market trend is identified the company may not be in a position to take advantage of it. For instance, one company which developed a new product for car upholstery repairs eventually decided not to proceed with marketing because that sector of the retail market was outside their experience. In other cases careful budgeting may show that the demand for resources cannot be met.

4.31 *The marketing plan*

A marketing plan must contain:

(a) current marketing situation;

(b) data on, and an analysis of, the market, product, distribution, competition, and general background environment. The data should be as precise as possible and may include the following:

- *Target market*
  Including prices, sales, market share and expected profits.
- *Marketing expenses*
  Including the budgeted costs of promotion and distribution.
- *Long run investment appraisal*
  Including the cash flow effects of the marketing strategy, allowing prediction of pay-back and return on investment.

- *SWOT analysis*
  Data and analysis on strengths, weaknesses, opportunities and threats facing the business.

- *Objectives*
  Business goals, including sales (volumes and prices), margins, profits, market share.

- *Marketing strategy and actions*
  What will be done to meet the objectives ?
  When will it be done ?
  Who will do it ?
  What are the costs and returns ?

- *Financial Budget*
  Profit and Loss statements
  Investments required
  Financing
  Budgets

- *Controls*
  How the plan will be monitored.

  Clearly, the management accountant must ensure that the financial budgets are well founded and competently prepared. The report is usually preceded by an Executive Summary.

4.32 The product life cycle

The market potential and profitability of products change over time. The product life cycle identifies four stages:

(1) *Introduction*. At the introductory stage, sales are slow and markets and profits limited because of high investment and promotion costs;

(2) *Market growth*. At this stage, sales grow, markets are widened and profits improve;

(3) *Maturity*. At this stage, sales grow little, if at all. Profits stabilise or begin to decline and may be defended by heavy marketing expenditures or the products may be regarded as 'cash cows' to be milked whilst resources are concentrated on 'new stars'.

(4) *Decline*. At this stage, the product begins to lose its appeal in the face of competing new products, changing public taste and fashion; sales decline, the market contracts and profits fall.

The typical life cycle pattern is thus an S-shaped curve. It is assumed that some products entering the decline stage may be relaunched, which means putting them through the development process afresh. This yields a life cycle pattern with two 'humps'. If there are repeated launches as new applications, new markets, and/or new users are found, the result is a 'scalloped' pattern. These stages are arbitrary, and researchers have identified up to seventeen different life cycle patterns, but the idea of the life cycle does highlight the need to continuously review:

- sales performance of all products;
- profit performance of all products;
- marketing, production and purchasing policies.

4.33 *The ideal product life cycle*

New product strategies are based on a forecast product life cycle. Ideally, the company may hope that:

(a) the initial development period will be short and that costs can be restrained in this period;

(b) the introduction/growth period will be short, with sales reaching their peak quickly;

(c) the maturity period will last a long time during which all development costs and introduction losses will be recouped and be followed by stable, high, profits;

(d) decline will be gentle when it comes.

These conditions are more easily achieved by consumer products than by high technology products. Again, the message is that realism should prevail.

4.34 *Competitive stages*

Three competitive stages in the development of a product market may be identified:

Stage 1

The product pioneer is the sole supplier with 100 per cent of the market and production capacity.

Stage 2

(a) Competitors penetrate the market and leader's share of market and production capacity fall, but sales and production volumes may still be rising as the market grows.

(b) Competitors may set lower prices which customers may perceive as reflecting risks of uncertain quality.

(c) The leader loses perceived quality premium and with it any price premium.

(d) Capacity becomes too large for the market and margins decline, thus keeping out new entrants and leading to Stage 3.

Stage 3

(a) Market shares, prices and production capacity stabilise.

(b) Some competitors may withdraw and the market leader may drive for a higher market share.

(c) Rates of return fall to an average rate.

4.35 Price and promotion spending

The price the customer is asked to pay is related to the amount the company is prepared to pay on promotion of the product. Four strategies are possible:

(1) *high price/high promotion spending* ('fast-skimming' approach);

This strategy uses high promotional spending to:

- justify the high price;
- give rapid market penetration;
- build up brand preference before the entry of competitors;
- achieve early profit and cash break-even.

(2) *high price/low promotion spending* ('slow skimming' approach);

This strategy:

- gives high profit combined with low promotion costs;
- suits a small, price insensitive market insulated from competition.

(3) *low price/high promotion spending* ('rapid penetration' approach);

This strategy is advisable when:

- the market is large;
- large-scale production with falling marginal costs are obtainable;
- the market is new but buyers are expected to be price sensitive;
- early copying or imitation will lead to rapid entry of competitors.

(4) *Low price/low promotion spending* ('slow penetration' approach);

This strategy works best when:

(a) there is a large, price sensitive market;

(b) the market is not very sensitive to promotion.

4.36 *Type of sale*

Volume and prices may also depend on the type of sale effected, which may be:

(a) First time sales
In this case, sales volumes depend on the size of the total market and the share of market achieved in each time period.

(b) Replacement sales
These will depend on the life of the first product sold, whether it gives satisfaction, the availability of substitutes from competitors, market and fashion trends, selling effort, and so on. Some businesses ignore replacement sales until the product is well established and some clear idea of the market emerges.

(c) Repeat sales
Some products, such as food and drink are purchased repeatedly. Since the unit price is usually low, the rate of repeat purchase is an important determinant of sales volume.

(d) Spares
For some products, such as aircraft, the market for spares may be captured with the initial sale and may actually be equivalent to a further two or three aircraft sales over a future time period. In the case of most cars, however, the spares market is not usually captured entirely by the initial sale.

4.37 *Cannibalisation*

It is essential to judge the effect of marketing new products on the existing product line. New products may have some attributes in common with existing lines.

(a) All aspects of new products have to be challenged individually and in sum. For instance, where there are already three products and a fourth is introduced, the total contribution of all four should normally exceed that of the three unless there are strategic reasons for the fourth product to be introduced as a 'loss leader'.

(b) Marketing department may be asked to produce arguments for and against a new product.

(c) A new product may be tested for 'product steal' (i.e. the extent to which it will replace sales of other products) before launch as part of the market research at the test market stage.

(d) Management accounting department is expected to compute the results and to discuss the impact of these in detail with the marketing department.

4.38 Records of product performance

Records may be maintained in different forms and in different departments.

- Physical records may be kept by marketing.

- Accounts department may publish a monthly detailed statement of the performance of each product by customer.

- Agencies may be used to conduct market share surveys. One company does this every two months.

- The relevant departmental managers in sales and marketing may be informed through the computerised management information system of any adverse trends on existing products and are expected to initiate action.

- For some companies, it may be an essential part of their operating philosophy to have a substantial flow of information circulating freely through all functions. Such a philosophy would enable all departments, especially finance, to be interested and actively involved in all aspects of the company's activities. This develops a better judgement of competitive effects and opportunities. As part of this philosophy, one company interchanges managers functionally and globally.

4.39 Financial appraisal of new proposals

Financial appraisal will be conducted by the management accountant who should review the pricing, sales, cost and profit projections and compare the results to the business objectives. The incremental costs of the new product concept may be calculated, including the cost of cannibalisation of existing products, and the cost of meeting the capital requirements. The financial appraisal should be as accurate and comprehensive as the time available allows, remembering that a timely estimate is better than an accurate report submitted after the decisions have been made.

4.40 Financial statement for new proposals

A statement showing the profits and/or cash flows over an appropriate time period should be prepared comparing the forecast results to the business objectives and the targets set for new products. The form of the statement will reflect the organisation's needs, but will probably show gross profits, gross contribution, net contribution (after deducting or adding the effect of the new product on existing products/markets), and the present value of cash flows discounted at the company's criterion rate. Table 4.2 is an example.

Table 4.2
Five-year projected profit and cash flow statement
in £ million

Item	Year					
	0	1	2	3	4	5
Sales revenue	0	22	33	46	72	94
Cost of goods sold	0	6	10	15	25	28
Gross margin	0	16	23	31	47	66
Development costs	8	0	0	0	0	0
Marketing costs	2	20	18	16	20	20
Head office overhead	1	2	2	3	4	6
Contribution from product	−11	− 6	3	12	23	40
Contribution on related products	− 2	4	4	6	6	5
Net attributable contribution	−13	− 2	7	18	29	45
PV (discounted at 16 per cent)	−13	−2	5	11	16	21

4.41 *Costs of new proposals*

Proposals will normally involve two types of cost:

(a) *Development costs*

Development costs are of three types:

- *Prototype development* – the costs of producing and testing prototypes of the products.
- *Marketing development* – the costs of assessing market response and producing the marketing plans.
- *Production development* – the costs of planning, designing and implementing production facilities, insofar as these are not capitalised as fixed and current assets.

(b) *Marketing costs*

Marketing costs include such items as:

- sales force;
- advertising and promotions;
- marketing research;
- marketing administration.

4.42 *Price and margin analysis*

In preparing the marketing budget, an analysis of the extent to which the end-user price of products is increased or reduced prior to their ultimate consumption may be prepared. The analysis should cover all significant brands and products and show incomes, costs, and mark-ups in total. When married to the predicted volumes, this will show the unit costs and returns. The level of accuracy of the mark-ups and consumer expenditures may need specialist marketing consideration. Forms 11.1 and 11.16 are examples. Form 11.25 is used for analysing 'downside risk': it shows what will happen to costs and revenues if sales fall below budget.

4.43 *Brand (product) volumes and market shares*

An analysis of the volume and market share of each product or brand may be prepared in which the expected sales volumes for each brand or product in each sector should be estimated. Local and special factors will be considered by the marketing staff, within the context of overall predictions of the total market volumes expected. The analysis will be broken down from a sales forecast or built up from detailed section or departmental estimates (or both, and then reconciled). Volume in this context can mean an estimate of sales revenues in money terms or an estimate of physical volumes, in which case prices also must be estimated. Form 11.30 is an example. A monthly phasing of volume sales, or, in a group, external volume by product, may be prepared so that closer comparisons of sales trends may be undertaken during budgeting. This type of analysis is particularly useful in businesses subject to strong seasonal and fashion effects such as leisure and entertainment.

4.44 *Brand (product) prices*

An estimate of the prices which will apply during the budget year is required. The starting point may be Recommended Retail Prices (RRP), from which allowances, discounts, VAT and other deductions are deducted to arrive at the effective price to be received by the company. The estimate may take the form of several price lists which show the prices applicable in each market or sector.

4.45 *Discretionary marketing expenditure*

Estimates of the advertising and promotional spending required to achieve the budgeted volumes should be made for each significant brand. The estimates will then be considered for an allocation of funds to promote the brand during the budget period. The spending will remain at the discretion of the marketing or brand manager to be used as required. Form 11.11 is an example.

4.46 Profitability analysis

The income to be received from all major brands and product groups can be built up by combining prices with the analysis of brand (product) volumes and market shares. The marketing contribution will show the income to be received less discretionary marketing expenditure. Several forms may be needed to analyse the contribution by product brand, market sector, department and section. Form 11.10 is an example.

4.47 New product contribution analysis

If the new product introduction is still under consideration a special new product contribution analysis may be required for each new product brand. The analysis starts with the face value contribution due to sales volumes of the new products at the product brand price. To this is added or deducted an estimate of the effect of the new product on the sales of existing products, *viz:*

(a) increases due to complementarity, e.g. increased sales of attachments when an additional power tool is marketed;

(b) decreases due to substitution.

Once the decision is made that the new products are to be introduced, these will be included in the normal budgeting forms with existing products.

4.48 Transfer pricing

The pricing of products traded between business units belonging to the same group must reconcile the need for optimum group profits with the desire of each unit to optimise its own profits. Agreed and consistent procedures for setting prices must be established and operated by all concerned.

5
Preparing Operating and Expenditure Budgets

The questions considered in this chapter include:

- How are operating and expenditure budgets prepared ?
- What is the value of the systems approach ?
- How do open and closed systems differ ?
- What are the characteristics of a good system ?
- What are the determinants of inputs and outputs ?
- Why is it useful to measure intermediate outputs ?
- How do we distinguish committed, programmed and managed fixed costs
- Why is the headcount a useful measure ?
- How can one budget for a salesforce ?

5.1 *Operating and expenditure budgets*

Operating budgets are sometimes defined as all the budgets except the financial budgets, that is, sales, production, purchasing, personnel, distribution, service functions and administration. For the sake of convenience, however, this book has dealt with the sales budget in a separate chapter.

This chapter is concerned with those operating budgets which cover the activities and costs of production processes and service delivery, including intermediate services and with expenditure budgets which provide for the costs of other functions. The distinction is by no means hard and fast. For example, transport may be run as a supporting service in one firm; for another, transport may be the main operating activity and a third firm may buy in transport on a contract basis. A fourth firm may own its own transport firm which it operates as a profit centre required to negotiate prices and contracts with other departments and companies within the firm. Each firm will budget accordingly, but it can be argued that the transport budget in all the firms should be basically the same if all other things are equal.

5.2 *Changing economic environment*

All advanced economies show a shift of economic activity away from manufacture and towards service industries. Within the manufacturing sector, the proportion of people employed in direct labour activities is also falling. According to *Cook, Burnett* and *Gordon*, 1988, between 1963 and 1983, the proportion of production workers in the USA fell from 72 per cent to 65 per cent. Whilst total manufacturing industry payroll grew from $100 billion to $395 billion, direct labour costs actually went down and constitute less than 15 per cent of total costs in most manufacturing companies.

5.3 New approaches

The current tendency in budgetary control is to establish measures of activity and performance for all activities wherever possible. This contrasts with the traditional approaches which emphasised the production departments and related costs strongly to direct labour.

5.4 The systems approach

The general approach now adopted is based on the systems idea in which an organisation can be seen as a network of interdependent components which perform various activities in order to achieve defined objectives. The system as a whole and each component within it can be looked at as a 'box' which accepts inputs, carries out some sort of transformation process and then yields outputs, as in Figure 5.1

Figure 5.1

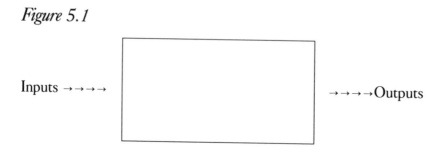

Inputs →→→→ [   ] →→→→Outputs

5.5 Open and closed systems

A closed system is one which automatically controls and modifies its own operations by responding to data generated by the system itself, like a thermostatically controlled heating system. An open system does not automatically control itself and must be supervised by people, who consider data on the operations and intervene to modify inputs, so that performance becomes satisfactory. Budgetary control is an open system.

5.6 *Characteristics of a good system*

Management accountants have long propagated the view that their information should *cater* to the needs of their organisation, that is, information should be:

- consistent;
- accurate;
- timely;
- economically feasible;
- relevant.

In addition, the system should:

- establish standards;
- define responsibilities;
- identify required actions and decisions to be made;
- porovide criteria to judge performance;
- identify points at which decisions are made;
- relate information to the decisions required;
- provide understandable information.

5.7 *Operating objectives*

Operating objectives must be clear statements of what outputs or levels of attainment are to be achieved by a component as a result of operating activities. The overall objectives are the production of goods and/or services but there are many intermediate objectives which can be used to budget for sub-components in the system.

Operating objectives are the basis for quantitative output measures. Not all objectives can be quantified precisely but even qualitative outputs can be assessed and levels of performance identified. The objectives budgeted for determine the amount of resources which will be made available for the component or sub-component.

5.8 *Operating measures*

Realistic measures of operating performance must be developed for each component in the organisation. These may measure outputs or inputs.

(a) *Outputs*

The first step must be to define the outputs required. What product or service does the unit produce? What are the results if it is successful? Who benefits from its outputs ? If outputs cannot be clearly defined or assessed, then it is not possible to continue, the component should be eliminated.

The nature of the outputs depends on the purpose of the component. A graphics unit may produce designs for posters, leaflets, video displays, etc. A transport section produces movements of goods and/or people.

(b) Inputs

The inputs to a component may be varied. The first need is for appropriate staffing. Then the accommodation materials and supplies necessary to support the work to be done must be found. From an accounting point of view the costs are normally classified as materials, labour and expenses. The budget staff must work out how and what inputs are required to the component to achieve the objectives. The cost of the inputs defines the amounts of operating expenditure to be put in the budgets.

For example, a graphics unit will require artists, art and photographic materials and supplies of paper, etc. A transport section requires drivers, maintenance and vehicle running expenses.

5.9 Determinants of outputs and inputs

The ultimate determinant of the budget must be the sales of goods and services to customers. What price will customers be prepared to pay and how many will they buy ?

An organisation has many intermediate activities which are indirectly related to its main functions of producing and selling its services and products. Intermediate activities are essential to survival but it is difficult to budget for and control the expenditures unless a methodical effort is made to identify suitable measures of performance and output for each one. These measures are related to the overall business and financial objectives even if the relationships are indirect. However many stages there are between the start of operations and successful sales to customers, the important point is that the ultimate determinant can be traced back through the system. It is then possible to identify intermediate determinants and output measures, which are related to every component. These determinants can then be used to allocate the input resource required and later to monitor and control performance.

For example, the number of posters and videos to be produced by the graphics section will depend on the plans for promoting the company's products. These plans will have been determined by the sales forecast and budget in which promotion activities are related to both prices and volumes of sales. The detailed sales plans should include details for a specified number of posters and videos. Thus we know how many posters the graphics section is expected to produce in the budget period. That is, the outputs of the graphics unit. On the basis of these outputs we can then calculate what resources, such as how many artists and what supplies, are needed. That is, the inputs for the graphics unit. To take another example, the outputs of the transport section are the number of movements which transport must make in the coming budget period. These depend partly on the volume and location of sales, as determined by the sales plan and budget, and partly on the involvement of transport in the operating activities of other components such as production. We may need to go to several other budgets before we know how many movements the transport section will be expected to make in the budget period. Once a figure for outputs is established, we can then calculate the performance measures to be applied such as the average size of operating loads, journey lengths and so on. The input resources will then be calculated, for example, how many vehicles are needed, how many drivers, and what must be provided for related expenses.

5.10 *Input and output measures in monitoring and control*

During the monitoring and control stages the output and input measures established for each component during budgeting are used as the basis for day-to-day management, since they provide the standards to which actual performance can be compared. Measures may relate to outputs or inputs or to a combination of the two. Control is dealt with more fully in Chapter 8.

(a) *Output measures*

- volume and value of sales;
- market share by product;
- volume and value of product sales by area;
- volume of production;
- number of units delivered;
- rejection rates.

(b) *Input measures*

- product costs by element;
- cost centre costs;
- head count by organisational unit.

(c) *Combined input and output measures*

- sales per square metre of store area;
- operating profits per employee;
- contribution to profits per unit sold;
- average margin per product, by market;
- sales per employee;
- administrative costs as percentage of sales.

5.11 Efficiency, economy and effectiveness

In setting budgets and monitoring performance we can assess:

(a) Efficiency

Efficiency is the rate at which inputs are converted into outputs, i.e.

$$\text{Efficiency} = \frac{\text{Outputs}}{\text{Inputs}}$$

(b) Economy

Economy is concerned with the price paid for inputs of the right quality or the conversion of finance into required inputs at the best possible price.

(c) Effectiveness

Effectiveness is the extent to which the outputs from a component or sub-component actually meets the needs of the user.

Arnold, 1987, says that all three factors should be considered.

5.12 Fixed and variable costs

It is generally accepted that some costs are fixed whilst others vary in accordance with production and/or sales volumes. Many overhead costs are recognised as being semi-variable, but these can be broken down into a fixed and a variable component.

The implication of the systems approach to the organisation and budgeting is that input resources required for any component or sub-component can be analysed as being variable or fixed in relation to the outputs of the component concerned. For example, some of the costs of a graphics unit, such as paper and film footage may be considered variable and calculated fairly accurately from the number of videos or posters to be produced. Others can be treated like fixed costs, such as staffing, where the number of artists employed will create the capacity to operate at certain production levels.

5.13 Variable costs

The starting point for variable costs will be to find the correct underlying variable to which the costs are related. Certain sales costs, such as bought-in product costs, will vary according to the volume of sales. Some production costs, such as material and component costs, will vary according to the number of units produced. Because levels of stock may change, sales and production volumes in the budget period may differ.

The budgeted volume to be produced and/or sold, or used as an intermediate output from a sub-component, is multiplied by the relevant unit cost factor to calculate the total variable costs, i.e:

Variable cost = total output volume x unit cost

In the early stages of budgeting, in setting guidelines, for instance, the budgeters may calculate a total for variable costs from the draft profit and loss account and use this to calculate a unit variable cost for planning and engineering use, i.e:

Unit variable cost = Total variable costs / total volume

At later stages, as the main output volumes for sales and production are set, and the corresponding subsidiary volumes for sub-components calculated from them, the resulting variable costs will be calculated and checked to see that they remain within the budget parameters. The effect on sub-components may not be in line with the overall output levels. For instance, if sales and production targets are reduced because of a declining market, one result may be an increase in sales promotions and the outputs required from the graphics unit may increase. On the other hand, the effect on the transport outputs required is more likely to be in line with the overall decline.

5.14 Component fixed costs

Each component may have some costs which are fixed, that is not varying with the activity of the component such as equipment and facilities. Nevertheless, these costs can often be budgeted in relation to some other factor. For instance, the graphics section may need more furniture and working space and possibly more cameras if the staff increases.

5.15 Overall fixed costs

In practice, many sub-component costs do not vary in relation to overall production or sales activity and so will be treated as fixed costs in general breakeven or cost/volume/profit analysis. The fact that the costs of sub-components have been analysed as variable in relation to the outputs of the sub-component does not mean they cannot be treated as fixed in general. Administration costs are a good example. The measures of outputs established during budgeting may enable many costs to be treated as variable but from the general point of view they are treated as fixed. The same is true of many overhead departments.

5.16 Committed, programmed or managed fixed costs

It may be useful to distinguish between different types of fixed cost,
for example:

(a) Committed costs

Committed costs are long run costs which reflect the choice of a level of
organisation and size of plant capacity, and in the short term are unaffected by
actual sales and production levels, for example, depreciation, rates, and some
insurances. Committed costs must be scrutinised carefully when the budgets
are being set because not much can be done to change them during the
budget period so long as the firm operates.

(b) Programmed or managed costs

Programmed or managed costs reflect decisions during budgeting to allocate
funds to particular activities not related directly to sales and production, for
example research and development, advertising, training, administration and
accounting. The organisation finds it difficult during the first stages of
budgeting to decide on how much should be allocated to programmed or
managed costs, especially when there are rival claims. For example, the R &
D budget is often set as a percentage of sales revenues, or training
expenditures are set as a percentage of total expenditures. These rules are
hard to justify on logical grounds. The systems approach is to be preferred. A
feature of programmed or managed costs, however, is that the organisation
could always decide to cut back on these costs if things are turning out
differently from what was anticipated. For example, personnel costs can be
reduced in an emergency by redundancies or by not replacing wastage, an
advertising campaign can be cut or delayed.

5.17 Average fixed cost

Average fixed cost per unit can be used when determining the allocation of
programmed or managed fixed costs. The average fixed cost will also show
the effect of committed fixed costs on unit costs and margins when production
or sales levels change.

The average is calculated:

Total fixed cost / total volume = average fixed cost per unit

Although it is often criticised, the calculation is used to control the allocation
of costs at the planning stage.

5.18 Personnel costs

Personnel costs account for a high proportion of costs in most organisations, and it may be the single most important cost to be budgeted. The budget must identify all the costs arising from the employment of personnel such as:

- number of people employed;
- headcount;
- wages, salaries and benefits;
- employee-related payments.

5.19 *Number of people employed*

The total number of personnel to be employed in sales and production operations and in related activities such as packaging, laboratory, production planning and management, administration, engineering, etc. must be established, in detail, department by department and section by section. Forms 11.18 and 11.19 illustrate the type of record needed. The structure required to meet the sales and production plans for the budget period can be worked out using standard labour requirements. If average operative output is 1,000 units per year, then production of ten million units requires 10,000 staff. The figures must be finely tuned to take account of staff turnover and recruitment delays. For example, the operator staffing required may be 10,000, but analysis of past experience may show that because of high turnover rates the actual staff in post averages only 95 per cent of establishment. The staff budget may then be based on 9,500 in post or if based on the theoretical 10,000, the departments may be given authority to use the funds from unoccupied posts for recruitment of temporary staff or overtime.

A similar problem arises when departments apply for new staff posts and can only proceed to appointment after the budget is approved. There is no way a person can be in post on the first day of the budget. If the normal time delay is four months then in the first year only two-thirds of a person should be budgeted. Part-time staff and overtime requirements can be treated in a similar way and expressed as full-time equivalents. It may be desirable to limit the use of overtime and part-time staff within broad parameters e.g. overtime not to exceed 10 per cent of full-time staff equivalents in the personnel budget.

5.20 *Headcount*

Many firms stress the importance of the headcount, or total number of personnel, in establishing effective control. Overall, the output per employee is a broad indicator of productivity used, for instance, by car manufacturers who seek to increase the number of cars produced per annum, per employee. Retailing organisations regard sales per employee as a vital measure of succcess.

Similar measures can be used at lower levels for instance by calculating the number of components per employee in a department.

All personnel should be included in the headcount, not just production employees. In this connection, the employment of an extra cleaner or a new manager needs as much justification as the employment of a sales person or shop floor operative. See the upper section of Form 11.19 for an example.

5.21 *Wages, salaries and benefits*

All payments to be made to personnel must be listed and identified, departmentally and by section. It is usual to do this initially by grade or category of employee.

(a) *basic wages and salaries*

The appropriate wage rates and salary scales must be associated with each person or group of people employed.

(b) *likely pay awards during the budget period*

This is a sensitive item since negotiations may be under way and disclosure of the amount provided to cover possible increases could affect negotiations.

(c) *increments payable to administrative and managerial staff*

These are fairly easy to calculate, since the staff may be subject to standard scales and increments.

(d) *benefits, expenses and allowances*

Various grades of staff may be eligible for expenses such as travelling, car allowances, health insurance, baby creche, luncheon vouchers.

(e) *overtime premiums*

The amounts payable will depend on the budgeted proportion of personnel requirements to be met by overtime working. See Form 11.18 for an example.

5.22 *Employee-related payments*

The budget must include all costs of employing staff, which fall on the employer such as the Employer's contribution to National Insurance, pension payments, training levies, etc.

5.23 An example of budgeting for a sales force

One group requires subsidiaries to produce these output measures as part of the sales budgets. Figures for the proposed budget period are accompanied by corresponding figures for the previous budget and current actual. The information required is:

(a) Headcount

The total number of personnel to be employed during the budget period. All staff are included, such as:

- salesforce;
- technical and support;
- head office, administrative and clerical.

(b) Costs

In this context the relevant costs are personnel spending and sales spending per profit centre. The total costs are shown and split between significant categories such as:

- discretionary sales spending, such as advertising campaigns;
- non-discretionary spending, such as salaries and wages, pensions and national insurance, etc.

(c) Activity measures

For sales personnel, these include the number of:

- calls;
- journeys;
- active days in the budget period;
- customers for sales and service;
- outlets served for sales and service.

(d) Efficiency measures

These are key ratios calculated from the data on headcount, costs and activity. Some examples are:

- cost per head in the headcount;
- average calls per day;
- average sales per day;
- calls and sales per day as a percentage of overall average;
- analysis of calls by objective such as:

(i)   maintain market share,
(ii) promote growth of market share,
(iii) minimise investment.

5.24 *An example of production, engineeering and distribution objectives*

One major company requires subsidiary companies to summarise the key features and objectives in the production, engineering and distribution budgets. These are then reflected in the detailed estimates and budgets. The topics to be included are not standard. They vary from year to year and between different functions or sections.

Some topics which might appear are:

(a) distribution service level objectives such as product order processing times, percentage returns;

(b) product quality objectives such as percentage returns, level of customer complaints;

(c) changes in processes such as automation, work simplification, use of information technology;

(d) changes in working hours and methods;

(e) effect of capital expenditure projects coming into effect;

(f) maintenance engineering regimes;

(g) dependence on plans of other subsidiary or associated companies in the group;

(h) external factors such as skills shortages, industrial disputes.

The summary combines and highlights significant cost and performance factors which may have a widespread effect on the detailed budgets and estimates. Major factors will be shown separately.

5.25 *Estimating production volume*

A brewing company takes the budgeted sales as the starting point for estimating production volume. A statement of total output for all products is prepared and summarised into major product groups. As well as the general factors to be taken into account, the estimates of volume reflect stock movements and the technical characteristics of production such as different bulkings in the production and handling of bottled, keg and bulk beer. At the detailed level, supporting production schedules are produced and phased according to the length of the production cycle.

5.26 *Estimating production costs*

The costs of each profit and/or cost centre should be calculated showing the variable and fixed costs separately. The aim is to show how the major factors affect both the total and the average unit costs, so supporting schedules are needed for detailed build ups and analysis of minor factors to be aggregated. The summaries and analyses must conform on the one hand with the categories used in the profit and loss account, and on the other with the accounts codes used throughout the accounting system.

Calculations of variable costs may be needed at each stage of the production process, for example in brewing where losses occur between the fermentation vat and the ultimate bottle or can.

6
Budgeting for Asset Costs

The questions addressed in this chapter include:

- What distinction is drawn between asset budgets and capital budgeting ?
- What are the purposes of asset budgeting ?
- What factors determine working capital requirements ?
- Is depreciation relevant in budgeting ?
- How should one budget for assets coming on stream ?
- How does planned maintenance help budgeting ?

6.1 Asset budgets and capital budgeting

Capital budgeting is concerned with principles used for selecting and appraising proposals for projects and new investments. The principles and practices involved are the subject of a number of CIMA publications listed below:

Reference	Title
244	The Capital Expenditure Decision;
14	Justifying Investment in Advanced Manufacturing Technology;
444	Investment Appraisal – A Guide for Managers;
184	Capital Budgeting for Foreign Direct Investment;
166	Capital Budgeting Practices in Medium-Sized Businesses;
112	Capital Budgeting in the 1980's: Survey of Investment Practices in Large Companies;
125	Capital Budgeting in the 1990's;
105	Management Accounting Guide No 6 – Capital Expenditure Control.

The term asset budgets is used here to denote those parts of the short-term budgets which deal with the fixed and current assets to be employed during the budget period.

6.2 Purpose of asset budgets

Asset budgets serve several purposes to ensure that:

(a) all assets, fixed and current, are included in the budgets for capital employed by the firm;

(b) charges are made to operating and expenditure budgets in respect of depreciation;

(c) new assets acquired or coming on stream during the year as a result of costs to be authorised under capital expenditure procedures during the budget or earlier periods are included in budgets for the year;

(d) when new facilities come on stream that the related incomes and costs are included in budgets;

(e) related maintenance and repairs costs are recognised and charged to operating and expenditure budgets;

(f) the cost of assets includes replacements, improvements or refurbishments.

6.3 *Definition of assets*

All assets, fixed and current, must be included in the budgets for capital employed by the firm. The reader is assumed to be familiar with the accepted accounting definitions of assets. The definitions of assets for budgeting purposes should be in line with current statements of standard accountancy practice. For example, Management Accounting Guide No 3 (revised 1989), Accounting for Research and Development Costs deals *inter alia* with the capitalisation of some research and development costs and is revised from time to time in line with SSAP 13.

Current examples of expenditures which may give rise to changes in the definition of assets are the accounting treatment of leases and the valuation of company brands. Future developments might extend the definition of assets to longer term marketing expenditures, company image and service.

6.4 *Determinants of working capital*

The elements of working capital are debtors, stocks, cash and current liabilities. Form 11.22 shows a form used to analyse stocks and Form 11.23 is used to analyse debtors. Form 11.15 is used in estimating current liabilities. In deciding levels of working capital it is necessary to trace the links between income and expenditure and between the elements of working capital. The links will include:

(a) purchases giving rise to creditors according to the terms of credit obtained from suppliers and the day's credit actually taken;

(b) sales giving rise to debtors according to the terms of credit granted to customers and the day's credit actually taken;

(c) in general, the budgets for all stocks are affected by the policies adopted on the links from purchasing to manufacturing/processing to distribution and selling. In particular:

- raw material and component stocks link purchases to manufacturing requirements;
- work-in-progress is a function of the manufacturing or processing time cycle and the policies adopted to link various stages between raw material/ components and finished stocks;
- finished goods stocks reflect the final links from manufacture/processing to the customer including the distribution system;

(d) arrangements for receipts and payments in advance, stage payments and receipts from customers.

6.5 *Working capital budgets*

Working capital and the associated ratios are an important element in the financial structure of the firm, perhaps accounting for 30-50 per cent of total assets employed. The budgets should be based on:

(a) A review of existing policies and the way in which they actually operate. For instance, the official policy for debtors may be 30 day credit terms, but existing ratios may show that the average is nearer 60 days. The consequence is a considerable increase in working capital requirements.

(b) Realistic attainable levels for each component of working capital and the consequential ratios.

(c) A detailed analysis of working capital and cash flows, usually on a monthly basis. Because of the knock-on effects of the links to various elements of working capital, some changes may not be fully worked out until several months have elapsed. Obviously, these effects must be analysed within the budget period, but it is also desirable to extend the analysis forward into the next budget period until the full effects have worked through otherwise nasty 'humps' might be bequeathed to a succeeding period. Methods are discussed more fully in Chapter 7.

6.6 *Depreciation of fixed assets*

The information about depreciation is relevant in assessing total product costs and in determining operating profits according to generally accepted accounting principles. Depreciation will therefore appear in the financial budgets and in the related reports to senior managers. However, depreciation is a sunk cost and its inclusion in operating and expenditure budgets should be considered by the budget officer who will scrutinise the relevance of information about depreciation to the manager or supervisor of each budget centre.

Whether depreciation should be included in the operating budgets is not a simple question. At lower levels in the organisation, depreciation may not be relevant to many short term decisions and should, arguably, not be included in budgets or reports. On the other hand, a total cost which includes depreciation and the associated full cost price can be argued to be a statement of the pricing and costing policy, to be followed by operating managers at the lower levels, in which case it should be included in all budgets and associated reports. One alternative treatment is to include depreciation but report it in a way which indicates its special status as a cost.

6.7 Budgeting for assets coming on stream

Some new assets will be acquired during the budget period as a result of expenditures included in the master budget. These are usually fairly small amounts falling within the capital spending limits of divisional and departmental managers. Larger capital assets may come on stream during the year as projects authorised under capital expenditure procedures are completed. It is essential that the cost of all new assets is shown as capital employed from the expected date of acquisition or commissioning, as shown in the capital budgeting plans. Examples of suitable forms are Forms 11.8 and 11.9.

6.8 Incomes from new assets

The inclusion of new assets in the budget, from the time they come into 'ownership' of the division or department, means the budget officer must ensure that as new facilities come on stream the related incomes are included in the operating incomes and the financial budgets. There may well be a delay between commissioning the assets and realising incomes, but the budget should be based on the predictions used for justifying the project in the first place, unless there are strong arguments against this.

For example, a project scheduled for completion in March 1990 may have been planned on the assumption that it would start generating incomes in May 1990. If it actually comes on stream in July 1990, then the budget officer's first assumption is that incomes will start in September 1990. If the budgets for 1990 are being finalised in November 1989 it may already be clear that some delay in commissioning can be expected. If so, the implications of any possible delay should then be considered. If the product is a Summer seasonal one, it might be that incomes will not start until May 1991. In such circumstances the contract for the new facility may include penalties to compensate for income losses, or commissioning might not be accepted until March 1991.

6.9 Depreciation on new assets

The depreciation charged on new assets will depend on the organisation's accounting policies on depreciation of new assets. Suppose the asset costs

£500,000 and is subject to 20 per cent depreciation in the first full year and it comes into use for the last three months of the year. The depreciation charge may be:

(a) A proportional charge based on the first year depreciation; this would be one quarter of £100,000, i.e. £25,000.

(b) A full first year depreciation charge irrespective of how long the asset is in use; this would be £100,000.

(c) No depreciation charge made unless the asset is in use at the beginning of the year. This would be zero.

From a management accounting viewpoint, (a) is the preferred option.

6.10 Maintenance costs

The maintenance of assets should be undertaken on a planned preventive programme. Such a programme means the maintenance staffing budget and budget for supplies can be based on a known work plan of maintenance activities, and unexpected demands for large replacement expenditures can be minimised. Some maintenance costs, especially preventive, can be expected on new assets and should be budgeted for. In practice maintenance departments are not always aware of impending demands due to new facilities and can hardly be blamed for not budgeting for the resultant costs.

6.11 Repair and inspection costs

Repair cost should be budgeted for the period following the expiry of any related warranties and guarantees. Where assets are newly commissioned it may be necessary to budget for post-commissioning inspections before the time for rectifications by the contractor expires. The costs should be charged to the appropriate operating and expenditure budgets.

6.12 Replacements, improvements or refurbishments

Operating budgets must include the cost of replacements, improvements or refurbishments. Operating divisions should take primary responsibility by including the necessary amounts in their own budgets, but in consultation with the maintenance departments involved. Proposals may be submitted with an indication of whether the proposal is optional or essential. As stated in Paragraph 6.10, budgeting for these costs will be easier if there is a well planned programme of preventive maintenance. The costs may be capitalised, in which case the depreciation charges for the basic asset will be revised to take account of them. If the costs are not capitalised, they must be charged to the appropriate operating and expenditure budgets.

7

Funds Flow and Working Capital Budgets

This chapter raises questions such as:

- How are funds flow, working capital and profit budgets related to each other ?
- What are the treasury and risk management functions ?
- Are funds flow statements more useful than working capital statements ?
- When should funds flow statements be prepared ?
- What items appear in funds flow and working capital statements?
- How can funds requirements be analysed ?
- What period should be covered by funds flow statements ?How will working capital needs affect profitability ?

7.1 Funds flow and working capital in budgeting

Forecasting funds flow and/or working capital is an intrinsic part of the budgeting process. The funds flow and/or working capital statement is the third corner of the triangle of financial statements in which the other two are the profit and loss account and the balance sheet.

The funds flow/working capital statements combine all those elements of the profit and loss account and balance sheet (income, cost and asset movement) which will generate a movement of funds during the budget period. Forms 11.5, 11.6 and 11.7 are examples of forms used in this connection. The determinants of working capital and how to budget for them were dealt with in Chapter 6.

7.2 Funds flow and profits

Funds flow and working capital needs do not stay in line with business profitability. An expanding, profitable business may easily run short of funds in the short term. A declining business may generate surplus funds for which uses should be found.

7.3 The cost and value of funds

If funds are short, cash can be borrowed at an interest cost. If funds are in surplus, even for as short a period as overnight, they can be lent out and will attract an interest return.

7.4 *The treasury function*

Many large companies have recognised that especially in times of high interest rates a specialist can save or make significant amounts of money by managing funds. Treasury departments are given complete control over corporate cash resources. They may also take responsibility for the overall structuring of company funding including debt and equity funds and corporate tax planning. Some treasury departments report to financial directors on funding for projects, dividend policy and investment appraisal. Some companies have established treasury departments as profit centres, although evaluation of their performance is difficult.

7.5 *Risk management*

Treasury departments may increase profits by effective management of funds flow risks, and efficient funds flow forecasting is essential for this.

7.6 *The purpose of funds flow and working capital statements*

As described in Chapter 3, the pro forma balance sheet shows the expected financing needs at the end of the budget period. Why then, is there a need for more statements ? The answer is that the funds flow and/or working capital statements show the *changes* in financing which have occurred between the two balance sheets. These statements assist in the management of financing by:

(a) identifying in broad groups all the increases and decreases in funds which will occur during the budget period;

(b) facilitating comparisons which explain why and how the closing balance sheet financing needs arise;

(c) clarifying the likely timing of cash deficits and surpluses when the funds flow is phased, by quarter, month (as in Forms 11.6 and 11.7) or week;

(d) disclosing peaks and troughs within the budget period when phased;

(e) determining whether cash needs are of a short or long-term nature;

(f) supporting decisions on the forms of financing to be used;

(g) improving profitability by optimising funds sources and uses.

7.7 *When funds flow statements are prepared*

Funds flow statements should be prepared whenever profit and loss accounts and balance sheets are prepared. Form 11.5 is an example. The first draft funds flow should be made when the implications of the guideline objectives are being worked out. Drafts should be prepared at each stage as budgeting proceeds. Early drafts will be for the whole budget period. As detailed budgets are prepared it will be possible to prepare phased budgets showing quarterly, monthly and/or weekly funds flows.

7.8 *Should you prepare funds flow or working capital statements ?*

(a) *Funds flow statements*

In the funds flow statement, the profit before tax is adjusted back to a cash basis adding back non-cash items such as depreciation and provisions to give the funds generated from operations. This balance is then adjusted for the changes in working capital and the additions to, and disposal of, fixed assets and investments. This shows whether the closing funds will be in deficit or surplus. When the funds flow is phased to take account of seasonal variations and the special characteristics of specific items, the result discloses what funds will be available or required to run the business, and when. Knowledge of both the amount and timing of cash funds needed can be critical to maintain liquidity and ensure survival of the firm during the budget period and beyond. Since it presents both short and long-term movements of funds, the funds flow statement is generally the best form to use in budgeting.

(b) *Working capital statements*

Working capital statements start with the opening balance of net current assets (cash plus debtors plus stocks, less current liabilities i.e. the short-term funds in use). Only the *long term* sources are added and *long term* applications deducted to finish with the closing balance of working capital. An increase in working capital at the end of the budget period indicates a shift towards short-term funding, but the main value of the statement is to show the changes that have occurred in long-term funding. Because the working capital is treated as one item, the emphasis of this statement is on the long-term funding needs of the business. The limitation of the working capital form of statement is that it may conceal undesirable trends in the make up of working capital such as an increase in stocks and a decrease in cash, which are movements typical of a dangerous under-achievement of sales targets. This form of statement is used mainly in financial planning and is of limited value in budgeting.

7.9 *Categories of funds flow*

A relevant list of categories of funds must be established. These are normally the same as those used in the profit and loss account and balance sheet although some additional explanation may be needed.
(See Paragraph 3. 16 on the need for standard definitions).

7.10 *Items in the funds flow statement*

In preparing the funds flow statement the items required are:

(A) *Cash balances*

Cash is defined as in the balance sheet and may include:

- bank current and deposit accounts;
- bank overdrafts and loans;
- government securities realisable within one year and not held for long-term investment purposes;
- building societies;
- short-term deposits with other companies in the group or to associates.
  As with the balance sheet, items such as overdrafts should not be netted off against other balances such as deposit accounts unless the bank has the right of set-off.

(B) *Short-term sources*

Short-term sources of funds are added to the opening cash balance. The main short-term sources are:

(a) A fall in debtors; a phased monthly analysis of debtors should be prepared along the same lines as Form 11.23.

(b) A fall in stocks; Form 11.22 is a phased monthly analysis of stocks.

(c) An increase in current liabilities such as trade creditors; Form 11.15 is a phased monthly analysis of current liabilities.

(d) Non-operational receipts such as dividends or interest should be shown in the funds flow statement unless the amounts are immaterial, in which case they may be lumped with funds flow from operations. Alternatively, a miscellaneous category may be established and supported by a detailed schedule. Care is needed to avoid double counting in group situations. Form 11.13 gives some examples.

(e) Receipt of taxes such as VAT.

(C) *Short-term applications*

Short-term applications are deducted from the funds balance. Short-term applications mirror the short term sources viz:

(a) an increase in debtors;

(b) an increase in stocks;

(c) a reduction in current liabilities.

(d) payment of dividends and interest;

(e) payment of taxes including Advance Corporation Tax and VAT.

(D) *Long-term sources*

The main long-term sources of funds are:

(a) *Funds generated by operations*

It is necessary to calculate the funds generated by operations and various methods can be used. One way is to calculate the figure from the profit on operations plus depreciation and other provisions. All these terms need to be carefully defined. For example:

- *Profit on operations*. Various definitions of profit are obtained at appropriate stages in the profit and loss account pro forma. The most relevant figure here is net profit on operations, that is margin on manufacturing less other fixed costs. Using the figure of profit before tax would imply that interest is not shown separately in the funds flow computation.

- *Depreciation*. The figure for total depreciation provisions charged in the profit and loss account during the budget period, including depreciation on disposals, must be obtained from the profit and loss account.

- *Non-trading provisions*. The net amount of all other provisions charged to or released from the profit and loss account should be calculated and added back to profit on operations, in addition to depreciation.

Another method is to calculate revenue less charges requiring funds. Defining revenue may be easy enough, but the figure for 'charges requiring funds' might be complicated to obtain. The simplest method is preferred.

(b) *Sales of fixed assets*

These disposals should be reported in the same categories as the balance sheet and will include sales of:

- plant and equipment;
- land and buildings;
- holdings in subsidiary companies;

- holdings in associate companies.
- license rights.

  The relevant funds flow is the cash proceeds from sale, but the net book value at time of disposal may be reported separately from the profit/loss on disposal. The disposals should be taken irrespective of whether the proceeds have been received or are still receivable. If receivable, the amounts are included in debtors.

(c) Issue of equity

This category will be used as the need for long term funds is established and decisions on long term financing are made. Subdivisions for various forms of shares may be needed.

(d) Long-term borrowings

This category is similar to the previous one. It will be used once a decision on financing has been made. Again, several categories of borrowing may be used.

(e) Government grants

A decision must be taken on whether to present this item as a source or to net it present against the appropriate assets purchased as a reduction of long-term applications.

(E) Long-term applications

Long-term applications mirror the long term sources and include:

- redemption of long term debt;
- redemption of equity by buy back of shares;
- purchase of fixed assets;

  The most important items here are capital projects approved and carried forward into the budget year. Forms 11.8 and 11.9 illustrate suitable forms for producing the required data.

- support for loss making operations.

  Forms 11.5 to 11.7 show suitable layouts for annual budgeting and monthly control statements.

7.11 Items in the working capital statement

The working capital form of statement will commence with a declaration of net working capital, that is, current assets minus current liabilities. To this is added the *long-term* sources and applications of funds (as in the funds flow statement). The statement concludes with the expected closing balance of net working capital at the end of the budget period.

7.12 Net working capital

The net working capital is current assets less current liabilities. All the items of working capital will follow the balance sheet definitions. The main items will be:

(a) Current assets

- cash;
- stocks;
- debtors.

(b) Current liabilities

- trade creditors;
- expense creditors;
- maturing elements of long-term borrowing.

7.13 Funding requirements

If the funds flow or working capital budgets indicate a need for more funds at some stage in the budget period or beyond, the treasury department or the equivalent personnel will decide on the best arrangements. There may be numerous alternatives but the decision-makers will need to know:

(a) What is the highest and lowest level of finance likely to be required ?

(b) Is there an underlying trend and, if so, up or down ?

(c) How long will peaks and troughs last and how do they compare in magnitude to the central tendency ?

(d) How do the projected funding requirements compare in magnitude to what was needed in the previous period ?

Comparisons may be assisted by a graph plotting the needs over the current and the budget periods.

7.14 Agreement with balance sheet

At all stages of budgeting, the additional long-term financing figure shown in the cash budget should agree with the long-term financing needs figure in the balance sheet. As some of the financing needs are eliminated by fine tuning the working capital requirements, or as decisions on long-term financing are made, the funds flow budgets should be updated accordingly with the balance sheet. As decisions to issue debentures or equity are made, the amounts involved are shown as sources under the appropriate sub-headings.

7.15 *Analysis by providers of funds*

The treasury department will anticipate the analysis likely to be made by potential providers of funds which will compare:

(a) company profitability and key financial ratios to industry norms or norms for the size of firm;

(b) the effects of borrowing on the company debt equity ratio and the ratios for comparable firms;

(c) the company business conditions forecasts with key indicators and market conditions;

(d) the track record of the company in all aspects, including its ability to forecast its cash needs.

7.16 *Providers of funds*

The funds will be obtained from the cheapest source which may also depend on the term over which funds are needed. Normally, short-term funds are cheaper but more volatile. Long-term borrowing is normally more expensive but gives certainty to the interest payments and capital repayment commitments.

7.17 *The funds flow budget period*

In general, the funds flow budget should be prepared for a succession of short periods, say monthly, as shown in Forms 11.6 and 11.7. As stated in Chapter 6, the knock-on effects make it advisable to carry the funds budget beyond the budget period, at least for a further three months. For treasury department planning a weekly or even daily period may be used.

7.18 *The knock-on effect on working capital and cash balances*

The movement in cash balances is dependant on receipts from income and realisations and payments for expenses and assets. Each element of working capital is dependent on other factors in business operations.

The links involved were looked at in Chapter 6. Because the use of funds for working capital is an important area requiring tight financial and operational control, continuous monitoring of the linking relationships is needed to determine areas where improved control and/or procedures will bring about a reduction in working capital and thereby a decrease in funding requirements.

7.19 *Working capital and profitability*

An increase in debtors, reduction in creditors, increase in stocks or increase in cash holdings all imply a net increase in assets employed by the firm. Unless these changes are accompanied by an increase in profits, then profitability will decline.

7.20 *The timing effects on working capital*

It is apparent that there is a time delay between the causal event and the resulting changes in working capital. For instance, an increase in purchase in period 1 results in an increase in creditors in period 2 or even period 3. There will then be a decrease in cash in period 3 or 4, depending on the terms of payment. Some contracts require payments in advance, in which case cash may reduce in period 1 before stocks rise in period 2 or 3. These time-based relationships must be built into the formulae on which the funds flow or working capital budgets are calculated.

8

Performance Monitoring and Control

This chapter is concerned with questions such as:

- What are the purposes of performance monitoring and control ?
- At what points should control be established ?
- With what other control systems should budgetary control be integrated ?
- What tasks, objectives and information can be identified as required in budgetary control ?
- How can a chief executive 'drill down' in responsibility accounting ?
- How do flexible budgets affect compliance with accounting standards ?
- What variances may be hidden ?
- How can forecasts be combined with actuals and budgets in control ?
- When are budget review meetings needed ?
- How can non-financial performance be monitored ?

8.1 Performance monitoring

Performance monitoring is an important element in managerial accountability and generally involves comparing actual to budgeted performance so as to see as quickly as possible where and when the operation is going off course.

8.2 Performance control

Control is established by considering the meaning of any deviations from budget and taking corrective actions, if appropriate. Where the deviation is beneficial, no corrective action is required but examination of the causes of the improvement may suggest other elements in the operations which could benefit from the same improvement.

8.3 The purposes of performance monitoring and control

The purposes of performance monitoring and control are to:

- fulfil the business strategy;

- establish control points;
- control expenditure;
- control profits and losses, and use of assets and cash flow.

8.4 Fulfilling the business strategy

The performance monitoring provides continuous quantitative tests as to whether strategy is being or can be achieved. It provides the information on which to plan and control tactical moves within the overall strategy. It assists decision making with regard to whether new opportunities will assist or detract from plans.

8.5 Establishing control points

Budgets are established and controlled at the most significant points in the organisation where the exercise of discretion is allied to accountability for decisions.

8.6 How budgets control expenditure

Budgets help to control expenditure by:

- requiring prior approval;
- relating all spending to agreed plans and objectives;
- monitoring and reporting on whether actual spending is in line with the agreed budgets;
- where flexible budgets are used, the variable costs are increased or decreased in line with increases or decreases in the outputs actually obtained.

8.7 Controllable costs

At each level of the organisation, budget formats should separate those costs and revenues which are controllable at that level from those which are not. The budget which each person is given must reflect the costs, revenues and assets for which that person is actually responsible.

For example, a manufacturing budget may include allocated costs such as depreciation or charges for services such as computing which are correctly required for total product costs. The manager cannot be held responsible if costs of this kind diverge from budgeted levels because (s)he has no direct control over them.

In a retail chain, the branch budgets may include rent, or notional rent charged, in order to calculate branch profitability, but the branch manager is not held responsible for that cost since (s)he has no control over it. Form 11.21 is an example.

As results and costs are consolidated upwards, there is always a higher level at which more senior management is responsible.

8.8 *Control of profits and balance sheet*

The financial reports summarise the financial results actually being achieved, compared to budget. All problems affecting the business may be assumed to ultimately affect the profits and balance sheet so the comparisons of actuals to budgets will provide early warnings of adverse developments. Some general problems affecting profitability, liquidity and asset deployment include:

- sales shortfalls due to products in decline;
- poor sales due to new products;
- production shortfalls or surpluses leading to stock deficiencies or surpluses;
- poor sales due to loss of outlets and inefficient distribution;
- lack of control of asset use;
- the effects of fiscal or environmental changes on trading conditions.

8.9 *Control of funds flows*

All problems affecting the profits and balance sheet will also affect the funds flow budget but the timings may be quite different. Some adverse developments may lead to improvements in funds position and some favourable developments such as increasing sales can lead to an initial deterioration of funds position.

Funds flow budget/actual comparisons are needed to provide:

- a continuous watch on the rate and timing of funds flows;
- a warning of deteriorating funds due to overtrading;
- control over flows of funds to and from budget centres;
- more effective management of cash by the treasury function, overnight or in the longer term;
- control of overseas funding and movements of cash across frontiers and between currencies.

8.10 *Responsibility accounting*

Classical management theory assumes that when managers are given the authority to act they accept the responsibility for taking the necessary actions themselves or through delegation. In unison with authority and responsibility is managerial accountability of which budgetary control can be a valuable part. In responsibility accounting, reports are submitted to those people who have accepted responsibility for costs, revenues and assets, in line with their position in the organisation. In general, the factors to which personnel relate tend to be non-financial at the lower levels, for instance a foreman may need information solely on budgeted, standard and actual hours worked/produced, or a salesman on numbers sold. At the higher levels, managers become responsible for cost and profit centres and it is more important for the accounting to be financially orientated so that comparisons may be made across the group. The fact that the vertical hierarchy is combined with horizontal product, regional and functional divisions creates difficulties in reporting variances.

8.11 Drilling down

In responsibility accounting, the chief executive is provided with a report summarising the results of his subordinates. The subordinates are given more detailed reports related to their own area of responsibility. If the chief executive wants to find out the basic causes of variances the system allows him to 'drill down' into the supporting detail and find out exactly where the problems are located.

8.12 Integrated control systems

The budgetary control system is only one of many systems through which management directs the organisation and it should be integrated with these other systems. For example:

(a) Control of sales and production

In this aspect of control, managers are using resources to achieve target levels of activity which are intended to attain budgeted profitability targets, or better. Variances should report on the physical inputs and outputs as well as on the associated costs and benefits.

(b) Financial accounting controls.

In this aspect, controls are established over expenses and accounting policies, and budgetary control could be asked to measure the effectiveness of the detailed instructions issued. With accounting policies compliance, it may be necessary to show reconciliations between the valuations used for budgets and those required by the accounting policies.

8.13 Performance control relevance

Performance control must be relevant to both the people who control and those who are controlled. The former can generally be provided with summary information, but the latter will require detailed breakdowns of the factors contributing to the performance. The expectation is that the controller and the controlled will discuss deviances from budget and agree on what action can be taken to correct unsatisfactory results. For example:

(a) A departmental manager may need a departmental variance report which compares budget to actual for each significant expense heading, plus a summary of key inputs and outputs, such as production volumes, head count and production hours.

(b) At board level, the performance reports will consist of a summary profit and loss account comparing budgets with actuals and an analysis of the variances by major department. Again, there will be a summary of key inputs and outputs, such as head counts, sales by product and market and production volumes.

The key factors affecting profits and costs at each level should be identified and reporting concentrated on these, rather than devoting immense attention to excessive detail.

8.14 Frequency of reports

Reports should provide feedback often enough for corrective actions to be taken. Supervisors and forepersons may need daily or even hourly reports. At higher levels, such as group, monthly, quarterly and half yearly reports may meet the needs of senior management.

8.15 Detail of reports

Actual results should be monitored against the budget and at the same level of detail. If the budget period has been phased into thirteen four-weekly periods, there will be thirteen reviews and reports comparing actual to budgeted performance in the budget period.

To meet the deadlines, it may be necessary to estimate some items. Where estimates turn out later to be seriously in error, it may be necessary to circulate fresh reports with the correct figures.

8.16 Timeliness

Comparisons should be carried out as soon after the end of each budget interval as possible and certainly within four weeks. Deadlines should be set for each report stating how soon after the end of the budget period it is to be circulated.

8.17 Need for reports and cost

All reports have a direct cost of production in the accounting department and they also have an opportunity cost to the persons by whom they are read. The management accountant must periodically examine and review the need for, and use of, all reports. Redundant reports should be axed. One approach is to prepare a report but not circulate it, then see if any complaint is forthcoming.

8.18 Tasks, objectives and information in controlling budgets

Control on the basis of budgets involves a number of distinct tasks with differing objectives and supported by various sources of information. One company analyses them into six distinct stages, as follows:

Tasks	Objectives	Information to Achieve Objectives
1 Review variances.	To check on significant variances.	Regular budget control reports from budget centres.
2 Recommend or require action by budget centre.	Control costs and revenues.	Analysis of budget reports by budget centre.
3 Review of actions taken on variances.	To ensure that action requested on variances has taken place or, if not, that an explanation is received.	Regular reports from budget centres as to action taken on variances or further explanations concerning them.
4 Feedback reports to planners, chief executive and/or board.	To ensure that effect of actual events on strategic issues is regularly and timeously compared with plans.	Comments in budget centre reports as to events affecting strategic issues. Budget appraisal reports e.g. from planners, as to effect of variances on strategic issues.

| 5 | Flexible or rolling budget adjustments – setting allowances – preparing, discussing & reviewing rolling budget adjustments. | To up-date systems based on flexible or rolling procedures in line with actual events. | Budget reports. Budget variance analyses Notes of budget revision meetings. |
| 6 | Budget audit e.g. by Internal Audit Department. This task is of particular importance in a computer based environment. | To ensure that the entire budget system is regularly checked to see that it is working satisfactorily. | System investigation reports from audit staff. Reports of system difficulties from budget centres. |

8.19 Comparisons

In general the classifications, forms and formats used in budgeting must be continued into the control process so that all variances are calculated on a strictly comparable basis.

Bases used in budgetary control systems are:

- actual for latest period compared to the corresponding budget phase;
- cumulative actuals against budget;
- past period comparisons;
- estimates and forecasts;
- ratios and operational comparisons;
- long and medium term budget comparisons;
- inter-firm comparisons.

8.20 Actual to budget comparisons

Comparisons of actual spending to the corresponding budget make up the main thrust of budgetary control. Any variance should be investigated and explained and remedial actions taken. Not all deficiencies are revealed by the comparisons of actual to budget during the budget period and other bases should be used as appropriate.

8.21 Cumulative figures

Cumulative comparisons are particularly useful to reveal underlying trends, as illustrated in Forms 11.27, 11.28 and 11.31. Another method is to use a thirteen period or twelve month rolling comparison. In Form 11.30, this basis is used to show total market and market share.

8.22 Past period comparisons

Comparisons with past periods may be of value in demonstrating business trends, but they are only a guide for corrective action if it can be established that similar factors still apply. Forms 11.1, 11.3, 11.5 and several others show that some firms use this method at the budget setting stage to compare proposals to the previous year budgets.

8.23 Combining budgets and forecasts

During the budget period some companies combine the budgets and actuals with forecasts to achieve more realistic assessments of performance. One company does this in the following way:

(a) Actual plus budget

Using the latest known actual situation as the starting point, the budget figures for the rest of the year are added.

(b) Actual plus forecast

Budget holders are then asked to forecast what they think will really happen for the remainder of the year and this data is added to the latest known figures.

(c) Projected variance

The actual plus budget is compared to actual plus forecast, giving a projected variance.

This type of comparison can be seen in Form 11.27.

One company employs forecasts in this way two or three times during the budget period, not after every interval unless very serious adverse trends are under way. Forecasts need not be as detailed as that required when setting the budgets. The main purpose is to make use of management business judgements during the budgetary control process.

8.24 Ratios and operational comparisons

Since many ratios are used in budgeting, it makes sense to monitor them. Some examples are:

- sales to packaging costs;
- return on assets;
- journey miles ;
- rate of stock turn;
- margin on sales.

A significant variation in any relationship indicates the need to dig deeper into the performance of both elements in the relationship. The ratios used in flexible budgets are of particular significance since they are used to increase or decrease budget allowances. Operational comparisons should clearly relate to the way the organisation operates commercially. For example, a firm operating a distribution fleet will compare actual to budget:

- average miles per trip;
- average number of trips;
- standard load and unload times;
- distribution volumes;
- marginal business.

8.25 Long and medium-term budget comparisons

Comparisons of the short-term budget and actuals to medium and long-term budgets can be made for the factors which are common to both budgets, that is, the broader indicators such as profitability, market growth and market share. These comparisons are relevant to board and group levels

8.26 Inter-firm comparisons

Comparisons should be made to companies in the industry which are of similar size. Data may be obtained from published material, trade associations or through inter-firm comparison schemes.

8.27 Flexible budget comparisons

In flexible budgeting, the value allowance for variable costs is adjusted or 'flexed', to take account of the volumes of sales and production actually achieved in the period. Flexible budgets make it more difficult to comply with some accounting policies, such as a requirement that full cost overheads are included in stock valuations and used in calculating trading profits. Reconciliation statements should be kept to show the adjustments which have been made.

8.28 *Variance accounting*

Budgetary control is supported by variance accounting when the planned activities of the organisation are expressed in budgets, standard costs, prices and profit margins and the differences between these and actual results are compared and accounted for. The arithmetical difference is the variance. Budgets can be used without standard costs. It is assumed readers are familiar with the technical aspects of variance analysis.

8.29 *Causes of variance*

There are many potential causes for variances:

(a) *external factors*, e.g.

- economic, social, legal and political changes;
- changes in competition;
- changes in supply conditions at home or abroad.

(b) *internal factors*, e.g.

- change in operating systems;
- inefficiencies;
- change as a result of other budget elements which have altered e.g. stocks and debtors will change with sales, but so will production and sales expenses;
- poor budgeting can be responsible for variances, but accountants are generally reluctant to accept this explanation.

8.30 *Short and long term variances*

Variances may be due to a temporary fluctuation, for which corrective actions may be taken at the operating level, or to some more permanent change which may require actions at a higher level. For instance a salesman's failure to achieve his monthly target may be due to his failure to follow planned routes, for which corrective action may be taken by the supervisor when the deviation is detected. On the other hand, the variance may reflect a recession in sales due to higher interest rates, for which corrective actions, such as cheaper credit terms, would have to be taken at a much higher level in the company or group. General factors such as the effects of interest rate rises on the market might be reflected in a change in market share or a change in the total market. Ideally, a management information system should be reporting on these factors as part of the budget performance monitoring system.

8.31 Service department variances

With progressive automation there is a decrease in production personnel but an increase in service and specialist departments who may not be engaged on current production at all. As discussed in Chapter 5, it is feasible to establish output measures and performance indicators for these departments. The performance reports should be tailored to the departmental norms as established during the budget setting process. Even if the department as a whole is treated as a fixed cost, the reports may well report some costs on a flexible budgeting basis.

8.32 Corrective actions

A variance may show the need for action in two ways:

(1) Individual budgets may be getting seriously out of line and individual budget holders need to recommend and take corrective actions.

(2) A large number of minor variances in various small units of the organisation, insignificant in themselves, may produce an overall profit and loss, balance sheet and/or cash flow which is significantly at variance and unacceptable. Action will need to be taken over a wide front to exert tighter control.

Some variances may not be immediately apparent from direct comparison of actual to budget, for instance when sales have fallen a reduction of trade debtors should occur. If sales grant relaxed terms of credit, however, debtors may not fall. Investigation of the facts should lead to appropriate action. If the credit terms relaxation makes good sense, then the effect on cash flow budgets needs to be monitored.

8.33 Monitoring and reporting non-financial performance

Key business factors which underpin the achievement of profit targets for the company should be monitored and reported. Some key areas are:

(a) *Sales volumes.* These are underpinned by the total market and market share.

(b) *Manning levels and pay rates.* These are influenced by the general and local employment situations.

(c) *Supplies, components and materials.* These are dependent on suppliers who may be affected by pay disputes or materials shortages.

Commentaries accompanying monthly and/or cumulative variances should report on relevant general factors such as consumer expenditure, exchange rates or the weather.

Adverse variances should be explained first in non-monetary terms of the actions to be taken, and then the financial effects of these actions can be calculated. Where a cost or a profit measure is inappropriate, then a non-monetary appraisal must suffice.

Even though it is important to achieve particular non-monetary targets, eventually all actions must be related back to the achievement of a profit target. So care must be taken to ensure that achievement of a non-monetary target is not used as an excuse for not achieving the budget financial performance in sales values, cost savings or operating profits.

8.34 *Explanations and actions*

In all cases the budget holder, of the element showing variances from budget, should be asked for an explanation of the variance and recommendations for corrective action if the variance is adverse. All the explanations should be drawn together and reported to the budget committee. The committee should determine the actions to be taken and issue clear directives for implementation. Implementation should be monitored and reported back to the budget committee.

8.35 *Corrective action reports and follow-up*

Once decisions on corrective actions are made, targets should be reassessed and follow up organised to ensure that the reassessed targets are being achieved.

8.36 *Budget review meetings*

Feedback on the achievement of corrective actions can be considered at regular budget review meetings where the main managers involved are in attendance. On the shop floor, these meetings may be daily or weekly. At departmental level and above, they may be monthly. Minutes should be kept, with an indication against each item of the person(s) taking responsibility for actions. Each meeting should start with a report-back session arising from the minutes of the previous meeting.

8.37 *Reward systems*

The achievement of performance targets should logically lead to incentive rewards. For example, a salesman may receive a bonus for achieving budget sales, with further bonuses depending on the excess over budget. The scheme may include elegibility for competitive awards such as a holiday for two in Paris, for best performance in relation to budget.

Safeguards may be needed to ensure that financial performance is not at the expense of commercial performance, for example overloading stock on to retailers. There is a growing tendency to reward managerial staff, also, with bonuses. For example, half of the bonus may be for achieving budgeted profit or costs and half for achieving other targets such as sales volumes, quality improvements or improvements in safety standards.

9
Special Problems in Budgeting

Among the questions addressed by this chapter are:

- What is meant by Advanced Manufacturing Technology (AMT)?
- What is CAD/CAM?
- What are Flexible Management systems (FMS)?
- What is meant by Computer Integrated Manufacture?
- What is meant by World Class Manufacturing systems?
- What is the significance of Total Quality Control (TQC)?
- What are the implications of Just-in-Time manufacturing systems?
- How are zero-base budgeting and the cost management process applied?

9.1 *Advanced manufacturing technology (AMT)*

The immense advances in computer technology are a leading factor in the adoption of new techniques in manufacture which are changing manufacturing processes, management systems, product design and production engineering methods and which have collectively been labelled 'Advanced Manufacturing Technology' or AMT. AMT is characterised by a return to small batch, or one-off, production of complete products using flexible, 'all-purpose' equipment.

The flexible equipment used in AMT has short setting-up times combined with high quality and is expected to be consistent in operation, that is free of interruptions.

AMT operates at three levels:

- the stand alone machine or piece of equipment;
- the production cell;
- the fully integrated factory.

9.2 *New products*

The products of AMT are expected to be varied and sophisticated in design and concept, of high quality, available with first class service but low in cost.

Life cycles may be short. Not all the products are themselves electronic. According to *Coulthurst*, 1989, AMT was being applied in both the textile industry and by H J Heinz in integrated food manufacturing.

9.3 Main areas of advanced manufacturing technology

The main areas of AMT are:

- computer-aided design (CAD);
- computer-aided manufacture (CAM);
- flexible manufacturing systems (FMS);
- computer-integrated manufacture (CIM).

Industries in the UK that have been at the forefront of using AMT include aeroengines and automobile manufacture while a number of studies have indicated that AMT has been a key factor in the recovery of the textiles industry.

9.4 Computer-aided design (CAD) and computer-aided manufacture (CAM)

CAD is a facility with which products and components are drawn on a computer screen on which they can be manipulated.

CAM is a facility with which operating systems, part routes and control tapes for numerically controlled machines, and requirements for fixtures and tools, are worked out on the computer and simulated before production begins. The two are often installed together as CAD/CAM.

The Rover Group reported a three fold improvement in drawing office productivity after installing CAD/CAM. The company regards the creation of a common engineering data base as the single most important innovation in the motor vehicle industry in the past twenty years and expects to reduce the time taken to produce a new car design from seven to eight years to four.

A small engineering firm with less than 100 employees installed CAD/CAM to deal with thousands of sheet metal part variants. The time taken to generate a program tape for a turret press was reduced from two hours to ten minutes and customers may make design changes at virtually no extra cost. See *Coulthurst*, March 1989.

9.5 Flexible manufacturing systems (FMS)

This manufacturing system is organised into cells within which tool changing, workpiece transfer and loading and inspection is undertaken. The Yamsaaki

Machinery Company achieved a reduction in the number of machines from sixty-eight to eighteen, of employees from two hundred and fifteen to twelve and in production floor space from one hundred and three to thirty thousand square feet. Average processing time was reduced from thirty five to one and a half days. A manufacturer of coal cutting machinery claims a reduction in production leadtime for machining of castings from six to two months and a reduction of work-in-progress by two-thirds. Allen-Bradley's integrated factory facility in Milwaukee operates without work in progress or finished stock at the end of the day.

9.6 *Computer-integrated manufacture (CIM)*

Under CIM, computer systems are used for production planning, production and inventory control, the issue of stores and parts, assembly, inspection, marketing and accounting. The ultimate ideal is for all aspects of operations to be integrated and use a single common data base. IBM installed CIM technology in thirty five plants across the world. The German plants reduced cycle time on one production line from twenty days in 1983 to six days in 1986. Material turnover rate was improved from 8.7 to 25 times per annum. General Motors, however, reported less success in obtaining benefits from three highly automated factories.

9.7 *CIM and budgeting*

When CIM is implemented, the organisation's manufacturing budget could be produced from a simulation of the budget period performance, drawing on a common data base which would include all aspects of manufacturing performance.

9.8 *World class manufacturing (WCM)*

This title was coined by *Richard Schonberger* in his 1986 book. The name was intended to 'capture the breadth and essence of the fundamental changes taking place in industrial enterprises' and included:

- total quality control;
- just-in-time production methods;
- new methods of managing the workforce;
- flexible approaches to customer needs.

9.9 *Total quality control (TQC)*

Total quality control is an approach to product quality which has sought to eliminate waste and improve quality in all aspects of an organisation's activities so as to reduce costs and improve the acceptability of products and services supplied to customers. The demand for higher quality has been one of the principal driving forces in the new manufacturing environment.

9.10 Just-in-Time manufacturing (JIT)

As the name implies, the basic concept of JIT is that products are manufactured no sooner than they are needed. For consumer and industrial goods, this would be just in time for delivery to the customer when demanded. Since there is normally a chain of production leading back from finished goods to components and raw materials, JIT may imply that production is undertaken in anticipation of demand, as in traditional systems, or it may imply a change in marketing method so that production is not initiated until a customer order is received and goods are sold with a condition such as *please allow 21 days for delivery*.

JIT is implicit in service functions: a service delivery capacity is created to be available for use by the customer on demand.

9.11 JIT production method

A Just-in-time (JIT) production system is based on product lines instead of specialised functions. JIT involves the creation of a new manufacturing environment designed to overcome the limitations of previous approaches. In the past, the ability to hold high inventories obscured some long standing production problems. Elaborate inventory and production control systems directed managers' attention towards paperwork rather than to what was happening on the shop floor. The aim of JIT has been to direct the attention of production managers, supervisors and operatives to the engineering and human problems encountered in meeting demand. Staff work as a team. The production capacity is constructed of cells and controls are concentrated on the input and output points of each cell. Paperwork is reduced to the absolute minimum and production control and administration systems are eliminated together with much of the traditional cost accounting and reporting . There is no attempt to document all production batches or to calculate detailed variances and there is no elaborate accounting for work-in-progress.

9.12 Characteristics of JIT

Some of the characteristics which can be identified are:

- an ideal of zero stocks of materials and finished goods;
- a lot size as small as one unit;
- creation of a balanced production capacity with short set-up times;
- stable production rates;

- an ideal of perfect quality, zero defects;
- elimination of waste;
- a preventive maintenance regime which eliminates down times.

9.13 *JIT materials budgeting*

Materials are budgeted as a single raw-in-process (RIP) category which covers both raw materials and work-in-progress. The materials budget can be calculated from the expected levels of production and sales, product by product, using the bill of materials. Alternatively, a global calculation based on previous budgets, adjusted for price changes can be used.

9.14 *JIT materials control*

There is no detailed accounting for materials under JIT. Take-off order quantities are small and based on frequent, reliable deliveries according to tight schedules agreed with the suppliers. Raw materials and components are released from stores on the basis of bills of materials or they may be held in open access store in the production cells. Physical control of materials is exercised by operatives and supervisors. Usage variances are calculated only for the material quantities scrapped.

9.15 *JIT control of payables*

Some companies have eliminated goods received and invoice verification systems and simply pay creditors on quantities used as calculated from completed production. This corresponds to the normal method of calculating payables and the timings, as used in cash flow forecasts.

9.16 *JIT labour budgeting*

Under the JIT environment there is no need for a distinction between direct and indirect labour since all staff work as a team on production and maintenance. Indeed, all personnel may be treated as staff and remunerated on an hourly basis.

In any case, the proportion of direct labour in industry is steadily declining. *Cocker*, 1989, stated that in the metal working industries it was less than 10 per cent of total product cost and in electronics less than 5 per cent.

The following alternative treatments have been used for direct labour:

(a) abolition of the direct labour category and inclusion with all other labour in the labour cost of the cell;

(b) retention of the category but relating it to the cell times.

9.17 JIT total budget

The total budget can be constructed from the allowed manufacturing labour cost of the expected sales/production, product by product, or by a global calculation adjusted for price and efficiency changes. Within the total, a shift stowards indirect labour may be justified by an overall cost saving. For example, although the indirect labour may be more expensive, because more skilled, there may be corresponding savings on materials or improved efficiency.

9.18 JIT standard times

The standard times are established for the cell as a whole, rather than for each element in labour cost. Thus budgeting and control concentrate on manning levels and overall labour effectiveness.

9.19 JIT labour budgeting and control

An overall measure of labour efficiency is used for setting labour budgets and can also be used to monitor performance. In all cases, the calculation covers both direct and indirect labour in each cell. For budgeting labour requirements, the standard hours value of the budgeted production is calculated. The standard hours can then be expressed as a headcount of personnel in various categories. Each category is then priced at the appropriate rates.

For control purposes, some companies use the labour effectiveness ratio:

$$\text{labour effectiveness} = \frac{\text{standard hours of production completed}}{\text{hours worked}}$$

These companies have claimed that the ratio:

(a) gives a reliable indication of profit improvement;

(b) shows improvements in JIT;

(c) retains the benefits of standards whilst accurately reflecting the product mix.

However, it can be argued that it is better to use the labour budget measure of effectiveness:

$$\text{labour budget effectiveness} = \frac{\text{standard budget value of production completed}}{\text{actual cost of hours worked}}$$

This ratio reflects both the amount of labour used and the varying rates paid for that labour.

9.20 *JIT labour control reports*

Control reports are furnished to each cell showing:

- the staff employed, both direct and indirect;
- the time operated by each cell daily;
- the quantity and labour value of production.

From the above information it is possible to calculate and show:

- labour or labour budget effectiveness;
- time spent on each product or component.

9.21 *JIT overhead budgets*

Under JIT, many overheads are included in cell cost. The costs remaining in manufacturing overheads represent services and functions serving more than one cell, such as materials handling and procurement, cost accounting, building costs, etc. Where possible, the variable elements of overhead costs are budgeted by estimating the expected usage of each resource by each cell. For instance, from quantitative output and performance measures such as:

- the number of loads, products or components to be handled;
- the cubic volume of products or components handled;
- the weight of loads handled;
- the distances through which loads will be transported;
- the area of accommodation required by each cell; and so on.

Adjusting for any price changes, the budget may be estimated cell by cell or globally from the various factors which apply in the particular case. Measures of efficiency, such as the expected output valued in standard labour hours can be used to estimate the budget allowances.

9.22 *JIT overhead recovery and control*

Companies using JIT do not use direct labour as a recovery basis. What they do use are multiple recovery rates based on direct materials, cycle times and total direct costs.

Control is facilitated if measures used to estimate the budget allowances, such as cost of materials per standard hour of output, and usage of services by cell, are followed through and used as the basis for control reports.

9.23 Irrelevance of traditional management accounting

Maskell, June 1989, argues that traditional management accounting is inappropriate under WCM because:

(a) traditional management accounting reports are not directly related to the company's manufacturing strategy;

(b) financial measures are not meaningful for control of manufacturing or distribution;

(c) traditional management accounting reports are inflexible and do not meet changing information needs in the face of continuously improving performance;

(d) traditional management accounting reports are typically produced weekly or monthly and arrive too late for JIT which needs at least daily information on performance;

(e) traditional management accounting reports apply overhead burdens on direct labour which is inappropriate today and can lead to poor decisions;

(f) traditional management accounting reports may divert managers into wasteful and unnecessary tasks just to 'make the figures look good'. Examples include moving stocks about (on paper only), driving for production at the end of the period irrespective of quality, just to achieve targets;

(g) traditional capital expenditure appraisal, with its stress on cash returns linked directly to capital projects within a stipulated time period is inappropriate to investments in JIT which may be related to non-quantifiable factors such as more flexibility in meeting customer needs, delivery improvements, total quality improvement, etc.

9.24 Performance measures and control for world class manufacturing(WCM)

Performance measures used by Japanese companies who are at an advanced stage in using WCM are as follows:

(a) *manufacturing lead times*: how long does it take to produce a completed product of satisfactory quality ?

(b) *direct labour productivity*: what number of products are made per direct labourer employed ?

(c) *work-in-progress turnover:* how many days requirements does the level of raw in process represent ?

(d) *incoming quality*: what percentage of incoming components are rejected ?

(e) *vendor leadtime*: what time elapses between notifying suppliers of component and material needs and delivery to shop floor ?

(f) *indirect productivity*: what is the ratio of completed production to the indirect personnel ?

(g) *material yield*: what proportion of the materials delivered is actually incorporated into finished products ?

(h) *finished goods inventory turnover*: how many days sales requirements does the level of finished goods inventory represent ?

(i) *inventory accuracy*: how accurate are the reported inventory levels?

(j) *absenteeism*: what percentage of the direct and indirect labour force is absent, daily, weekly and on average annually.

9.25 *Incremental budgeting*

Many people and organisations work on the assumption that budgets will grow each year. The rationalisations for this may be to allow for inflation or to provide for 'natural growth'. Incremental budgeting is the general approach in Governmental budgeting but is also found in private industry, especially in indirect functions such as planning and research. The approach is criticised from the scientific management and the systems points of view because it does not relate spending to the work to be accomplished. It may also avoid scrutiny of all activities to see whether they are required or not.

9.26 *Zero-base budgeting (ZBB)*

Zero-base budgeting was invented by *Peter Pyhrr*, whilst at Texas Instruments, when the company faced a dramatic change in the market for its products and in the skills required from its workforce and management. In effect, the company needed to break away from the comfortable habits of incremental budgeting and start again from scratch.

ZBB starts from the assumption that levels of expenditure in a previous period do not justify continuation of that spending in future periods. All spending must be justified from scratch each year. ZBB is most useful in control of indirect, overhead activities.

ZBB requires the following steps:

(a) The fundamental activities to be undertaken by each budget centre are identified and the expected outputs determined. The reason for carrying out each activity must be identified: in some Governmental organisations certain statutory activities are required by law and cannot be dropped, but otherwise ZBB assumes that unproductive activities will be dropped, or given low priority.

(b) A proposed budget for each activity must be drawn up and divided into decision packages showing the amount to be spent if various levels of priority are established for the activity.

(c) Senior managers review the decision packages of subordinates and rank the packages and suggest the priority levels for which budgets should be approved.

(d) Final allocation of resources for budgets is made in conformity with the priorities established in the ranking process.

(e) Performance is monitored on the basis of the performance criteria associated with the level of budget approved.

Hyndman, 1982, quotes evidence for the success of ZBB in the 1970's. *Cook, Burnett* and *Gordon*, 1988, say that ZBB is not a fad but may have lost public interest in the 1980's because ZBB must be tailored to the organisation, and a sound grasp of the implications of the company's objectives and procedures is needed to handle ZBB's human and administrative aspects successfully.

9.27 Advantages of ZBB

The advantages claimed for zero-base budgeting are that it:

(a) forces examination of all current service and support activities in the light of corporate objectives and strategies, not just new proposals;

(b) looks for alternative ways of performing activities and eliminates activities which are no longer necessary;

(c) identifies the resources required to perform activities at various levels of priority;

(d) is effective in ranking all activities in terms of importance and securing optimum allocation of scarce resources.

9.28 Cost management process (CMP)

This is a variant of ZBB described by *Cook, Burnett* and *Gordon*, 1988. The name avoids the negative connotations of 'Zero-base', because no funding is ever zero, and drops the 'budgeting' because the process is more than just budgeting and it also uses modified procedures. Six steps are invariably carried out in applying CMP although their precise form may vary with the needs and circumstances of different companies.

Step 1 Identify the lowest responsibility level

Usually these are the first line managers who bear various names such as foremen, supervisors, and group head. They will usually supervise ten to twenty persons. The sections may be called decision units, performance centres or cost centres.

Step 2 Set objectives and activities

The decision managers propose their objectives by analysing current activities in the light of the planning assumptions of the larger organisational department to which they belong, such as the production department. Together with the superior manager, they identify major activities and volumes and this leads to a statement of objectives and acceptable levels of performance. The manager and supervisor should consider all alternative ways of accomplishing the objectives, including contracting the work out.

Step 3 Conduct supplier-receiver reviews

At the departmental level, the cross-impacts of each decision unit are considered. Key suppliers and receivers meet face to face to explain their needs and services offered and justify their costs. Unnecessary services are eliminated, cheaper ways of providing existing services found and needs for new services identified.

Step 4 Prepare decision packages

Each decision unit manager prepares a base package to cover minimal services, and incremental packages for other activities, listing personnel needs, cost estimation, stating key benefits and a statement of consequences if the package is not implemented. The base package must show reduced costs when compared to the current budget.

Senior managers prepare base and incremental packages dealing with managerial posts only. All managers involved meet again to review the packages and it is claimed that the quality of the packages will be high.

Step 5 Rank the decision packages

The ranking is usually done in several stages and there are several ways in which this can be done:

- Senior management lay down specific criteria.
- A weighting scheme is applied to the alternatives.
- The group performing the ranking may vote on final choices.
- A group consensus may be sought amongst the managers, at the level concerned.

The stages of ranking are:

- The first rankings are established in the priorities set by decision unit managers at the lowest responsibility level.

- The second ranking is performed within each department at a meeting of all decision unit managers under the chairmanship of the departmental manager.

- The third ranking is set at an inter-departmental meeting at which all managers within a function or division meet under the chairmanship of the senior manager to whom they report.

- The number of subsequent rankings depends on the organisation and how many levels of management it has.

- The highest level of executive rankings are set by the senior executive managers for submission to the board as part of the proposed master budget.

Step 6 Make the funding decision

The final rankings and funding decisions are made by the board which is presented with packages summarising the staffing and resource requirements and costs for each division or department. The board may need to consider packages lying near the cutoff point, and re-rankings may be made after discussion of the consequences of non-approval.

9.29 Outcome of ZBB and CMP

The outcome of both CMP and ZBB will be a detailed operational plan and master budget for the budget period showing the funds allocated for the priority levels approved for each decision package.

9.30 Issues raised under ZBB and CMP

It is likely that various policy issues will be identified during the budgeting process. These issues may include:

(a) inability of some managers to produce realistic plans;

(b) lack of communication horizontally between divisions departments and sections, and vertically between junior and senior levels of management;

(c) inequitable or incorrect allocation of overhead costs;

(d) gaps in information about activities and the objectives, if any, that they serve;

(e) outdated and mutually inconsistent policies;

(f) gaps in the policies and the need for new ones;

(g) skill deficiencies and the need for training;

(h) shortcomings in the planning, budgeting and control systems.

(i) inability of accountants to perform the support and information role.

9.31 *Performance monitoring under ZBB and CMP*

Performance monitoring and reporting under ZBB and CMP will follow the formats established for the packages and objectives which were identified and approved during the budget setting process. The applicable budget will be the resources allocated for the approved priority levels.

9.32 *Additional resources under ZBB and CMP*

If additional resources become available during the budget period, they can be allocated to activities identified in packages but not initially approved. If sufficient funds are available for an across-the-board increase it may be possible to reduce the priority level at which funding is cut off. Similarly, if conditions change, the plans can be adjusted downwards without arbitrary across-the-board cuts.

9.33 *Advantages of CMP*

Cook, Burnett and *Gordon* claimed that CMP will help:

(a) reduce costs while maintaining or improving performance;

(b) create a bridge between planning and results by linking decision unit plans and budgets to departmental and corporate objectives;

(c) increase motivation by involving all levels of management in setting budgets;

(d) promote innovative thinking and proposals for change;

(e) improve vertical and horizontal communication.

(f) give top management an instrument for diagnosing the needs of the organisation if performance is to be improved.

9.34 *Disadvantages of ZBB and CMP*

There are a number of criticisms of ZBB and CMP.

(a) *Time required*
The time required to implement ZBB and CMP is likely to be greater than required for a conventional system, especially when the methods are first applied.

(b) *Paper work*
ZBB and CMP require a great deal more paper work than conventional budgeting.

(c) *Cost of budgeting*

Since both the time and paper work are higher, it follows that the direct costs of ZBB and CMP will be higher than under a conventional system. The indirect costs in terms of time and attention required from all involved levels of management will also be higher.

(d) *Subjectivity of measures*

ZBB and CMP are methods for applying measures to indirect activities which may be essentially immeasurable. The judgements made will be subjective and therefore inconsistent fluctuating from time to time and unreliable.

(e) *Dissimilarity of packages and rankings*

The packages ranked under ZBB and CMP are so dissimilar that rankings between them is inevitably subjective and no procedure will eliminate the necessity for judgements. Rankings produced by different sections and departments cannot be used to select between departmental and sectional proposals.

Proponents of ZBB and CMP will advance arguments against these objections. The case for ZBB and CMP is made in earlier paragraphs.

10
Examples of Company Budgeting Procedures

This chapter presents case materials from participating companies which illustrate how the principles outlined in earlier chapters are applied in practice. The first four sections are short accounts of how the budgetary control system works in:

- A regionalised newspaper group, (Paragraphs 10.1 to 10.6);

- A retail supermarket chain, (Paragraphs 10.7 to 10.14);

- A retail fashion chain, (Paragraphs 10.15 to 10.30);

- An aerospace and defence systems company, (Paragraphs 10.31 to 10.47);

  The fifth section is an example of company business and financial objectives taken from the published accounts of:

- An international food and drinks company (Paragraphs 10.48 to 10.50).

  A selection of forms used in the systems are shown in the next chapter (as Forms 11.1 to 11.31.

A regional newspaper group

10.1 Budgeting

The system used by this company is based on standard forms completed by business units and uses computer models.

10.2 Organisation structure

The group is composed of a number of business units which are called publishing centres. Each centre caters for a particular locality and market segment and is managed locally. Individual publishing centres prepare control budgets which are then consolidated into the regional budget.

10.3 Timetable and tasks in preparing group budgets

The timetable and tasks involved in preparing the budgets is set by regional head office, along the following lines:

(a) Beginning of August

The preparation of budgets begins in August when budget guidelines are issued by regional head office. The guidelines give information on agreed economic factors likely to affect market conditions. On this basis regional head office sets key performance ratios.

Standard forms are issued to publishing centres on which are prepared an estimate of results for the current full year with a projection for the budget year showing the achievement of key performance ratios.

(b) Mid-August

A first draft plan is submitted to regional head office by each publishing centre using the standard forms and giving details of:

- revenue;
- costs;
- profits;
- capital expenditure;
- cash flow movements;
- volume and price changes;
- staffing;
- taxation;
- key ratio achievements.

A commentary supporting the draft budget is welcomed by regional head office.

(c) End of August

Regional head office review the draft budgets under the following procedures:

- Directors receive the first drafts of centre plans before any adjustment is made by regional head office functional departments.
- The head office functional department heads review the publishing centre plans and report their findings to the board. The managing director of each centre receives a copy of the functional reviews. Directors also report to the board on the functional department findings.
- Each publishing centre plan and the functional reviews are discussed with a reviewing committee of the regional group directors and the centre management who then reach decisions on the final actions and results to be included in the control budgets.

(d) Early September

Publishing centres prepare revised control budgets and submit them to regional head office in early September.

(e) Early October

Regional head office consolidate the publishing centre control plans into a group control budget and revise the five-year strategic plan in early October.

(f) End October/early November

Regional head office submit the consolidated group control plan to the UK head office of the group, using standard UK head office forms.

(g) End November/early December

When agreement on the regional budget for the full year has been reached between regional head office and UK head office, the approved budgets are sent out to the publishing centres.

10.4 Performance monitoring and control

The first step in establishing monitoring and control procedures is that publishing centres calendarise the budget by phasing it across the months for the coming year. The calendarised monthly budgets are used for reporting against actuals throughout the year. Managers receive appropriate standard computer packages on a regular basis. Regular reports are prepared throughout the budget year comparing actuals with the monthly plan figures. For each quarter the forms show comparative columns for:

- previous year actual for this quarter;
- current plan for this quarter;
- current actual for this quarter.

Profits are re-forecast quarterly in April, July and September in quarterly periods but these forecasts are not used for comparative reporting purposes. The September re-forecast is used for the current year estimate during preparation of the budget for the following year.

10.5 Key financial factors

The key financial factors are revenues, cost and capital expenditures. Each factor is subject to quite different influences.

(a) Revenues depend upon the volume and price of:

- advertisements; *and*

- newspaper sales.

  Both sales and advertisement revenues are strongly influenced by national and local economic conditions and the state of competition.

(b) Costs depend on:

- the price of newsprint and volume of newspaper sales and the quotas between editorial and advertisement content;
- the wages costs which are a high proportion of total costs and require strict control over wage agreements and staffing levels;
- other costs relating mainly to inflation levels.

(c) Capital expenditure is related to:

- depreciation;
- borrowing requirements;
- effects on staffing levels;
- type of product, e.g. colour;
- elements of new technology being introduced.

10.6 Key business issues

Key issues were identified in early 1990 as various forms of competition, the impact of new technology, and the economic position of the industry, as follows:

(a) Competition is increasing from:

- freesheets;
- developments of nationals;
- local radio;
- television;
- specialist magazines.

(b) New technology has two main aspects:

- introduction of new computerisation;
- acceptance by staff (industrial relations implications).

(c) Economic position

  The economic position of the group depends upon:

- rapid and effective response to the local economic situation, such as unemployment levels, by the local Publishing Centres;
- movements in taste and demand for products affect the sources of advertising revenue and the content of editorial matter;

- publishing centres need to recognise and react to many specific local factors which affect individual companies.

A retail supermarket chain

10.7 Budgeting

This group consists of a large number of retail supermarkets. The budgetary control system is articulated with the long-term plans and makes use of forecasts, budgets and actuals to secure sensitive reaction to evolving market trends.

10.8 Relation of forecasts to budget

The budget is based on the forecast of the current year cost or profit. Current year forecasts are based on actual performance as far as it is available at the time of budgeting plus a forecast by the budget holder for the rest of the year. The forecast is usually closely related to the current year budget.

10.9 Relationship of budget to long-term plans

The budget is viewed in the context of a longer term three to four year plan drawn up at the global policy level which contains sufficient analysis of costs and profits for the budget to key into for comparison purposes.

The budget should broadly fit the long-term plan but bring refinement of detail for the year ahead and convert the policy document into a working operational plan.

10.10 Bottom up and top down approaches

Although overall guidelines are set, budgeting is essentially a 'bottom up' rather than a 'top down' exercise in the early stages. Only when the figures for all cost/profit centres are brought together to produce an overall picture is the 'top down' directive really imposed.

10.11 Budget guidelines

Budget holders are expected to consider primarily how to meet the requirements of their jobs using their own expertise to form their judgements and requests for funds. Budget holders are given general guidelines from head office on some basic expectations during the budget period. The factors affecting sales revenues and activity levels include:

- anticipated increases in sales for market as a whole and group market share;
- expected levels of throughput for the group as a whole;
- the number of items it is expected will be handled.

The factors affecting cost, capital expenditure and staffing levels are bound up with the factors affecting revenues and activities and are given special and separate attention. The kind of information provided is:

- the likely levels of cost of supplies;
- the likely levels of staff pay rates and awards;
- requirements for staffing and whether the labour market will enable required staffing levels to be met.

During the budget process, key indicators include:

- gross margin in relation to sales;
- net margin before tax in relation to sales;
- cashflow over the budget year;
- working capital ratios.

10.12 Financial statements

At each stage of reviewing the budget the effects on revenue, profit and loss, funds flow and balance sheet are considered.

10.13 Budget timetable and sequence of events

A draft budget is prepared in detail in the first instance by each budget holder responsible for an individual cost or profit centre. The budget period is one year. The budget process starts five to six months before the start of the budget year and the company think it is important that the process be concluded before the start of the budget year.

The company identifies five stages in the process, as follows:

Stage 1

During months one, two, and three of the process, budget holders incorporate and present in budget format their views on quantities of throughput, units handled and staffing levels. At the same time they produce capital expenditure budgets. By the end of month three both types of budget are formally considered by the appropriate board sub-committees. The resulting agreed data is the basis for *Stage 2*.

Stage 2

Further consideration of the initial guidelines may produce small refinements to the budgets but any changes are carefully monitored and recorded and can generally be made without too much reworking. Budget holders now put values on their quantitative budgets and bring in all other cost/revenue elements for their budgets. These are again formally reviewed by board sub-committees.

Stage 3

The agreed budgets coming from the board sub-committees are brought together for the first time in a total company package for consideration by the board. The package includes a number of schedules of detailed budgets compared with current year forecasts supported by narrative explaining increases or decreases, year on year, and stating assumptions used. The document falls into four sections:

- Revenue – profit and loss.
- Capital expenditure.
- Funds flow.
- Balance sheet.

Stage 4

The Stage 4 budget is prepared by estimating a value of various changes as directed by the Board. Various summaries of these changes are submitted to the Board for review and after two or three cycles the budget is finalised.

Stage 5

At this stage the budget is phased over the thirteen periods of the the budget year. Budget holders are then provided with budget reference documents showing each item of cost/revenue over the thirteen periods. Having been party to the compiling of the budget, they will now become responsible for it. Actual performance is monitored in each period against the detail shown in the budget reference document and significant variances are reported to the Board with the management accounts for the period.

10.14 Key issues

Key issues for this industry are:

(a) competitors' performance and their effects on factors such as gross margin;

(b) Government policy and performance on factors such as inflation expectations, taxation and allowances;

(c) availability of key resources and particularly staff of the right type and sites on which to build.

A retail fashion chain

10.15 Budgeting

This group consists of a number of retail fashion outlets. The system is tied into the five-year plans and budgetary control is highly developed with both annual and semi-annual budgets and performance reviews at Area, Regional and Head Office levels.

10.16 Budget period and financial year

The company budget period and financial year extends from September to August because this fits the natural business year in the fashion trade. In fact the year is strongly bi-seasonal and the budgeting system must reflect this.

10.17 Planning process

The planning process is highly developed and several plans are maintained at all times. Each type of plan is developed on a different basis because the company endeavours to maximise the use of the information available.

(a) The basic business plan is a five-year plan which is frequently up-dated. This is explained in Paragraph 10.18.

(b) There is then an annual or full year plan and budget which matches the company financial year, September to August and which is articulated with the five-year plan. This is explained in Paragraph 10.19.

(c) The company prepares a first half-year plan at the start of the budget year. This is extracted from the full year plan and budget and explained in Paragraph 10.20.

(d) The company prepares a second half-year plan once the first half-year is well under way. This is based on the full year plan and the actual results flowing in from the first half operations. This is explained in Paragraph 10.21.

10.18 Five-year plan

The five-year plan is a set of financial statements: profit and loss account, balance sheet and funds flow statement. These are submitted to divisional, sector and main boards three times per year.

(a) In November, the first year is based on a forecast first half plus the second half plan.

(b) In March, the first year is based on first half actual plus a revised second half plan.

(c) In July, the first year is based on first half actual plus a second half forecast.

10.19 Full year plans

Preparation of these plans extends from April to August and proceeds through the following stages.

(a) 'Like-for-like' sales increases are estimated in April using sales price inflation and volume growth based on key factor guidelines. The figures are determined by negotiations between retail operations, buying and merchandising, and finance.

(b) Plan guidelines are determined in May by negotiations between retail operations, buying and merchandising, concessions and finance.

(c) A sales plan for each branch is produced in May by negotiations between retail operations, concessions, and finance.

(d) Margins are determined in April by retail operations, buying and merchandising, and finance.

(e) Payroll and other branch cost estimates are determined in May by personnel, retail operations, and finance.

(f) Central services costs are estimated by departmental directors and finance.

(g) Full year profit and loss account, balance sheet and funds flow statement are submitted to divisional board, sector board and main board for consideration, amendment and eventual approval. This should be completed in May but may extend into June.

(h) The full year objectives are finalised by main board in July and August.

The full year increase will be split to give first and second half increases.

Details of first and second half openings, modernisations, closures and transfers are included. The figures must agree with the latest agreed sales forecast from the board papers (see monitoring below).

10.20 First half plans

Preparation of these plans extends from April to August and undergo the following stages.

(a) Sales phasing by week is agreed by negotiations between retail operations, buying and merchandising, and finance in April. Separate negotiations are held between concessions and finance. The plans are analysed by seaside resorts, city centres, central London, Scottish, Irish and other branches.

(b) Sales plans by branch are agreed by retail operations, concessions, and finance in May.

(c) Cost plans are agreed by branch by retail operations, personnel, and finance between May and June.

(d) Central cost plans by cost centre are determined by departmental directors and finance in May and June.

(e) The full year plan split by half year is presented to the divisional, sector and main boards in July.

(f) Final adjustments to the first half year plan may be made in August, immediately before implementation in September.

10.21 *Second half plan*

The second half plan is updated for first half actual performance, new information and proposed action to achieve profit target for the year. Preparation of these plans extends from December to February and goes through the same stages as the first half plan although the Christmas season affects the timing.

(a) Sales phasing by week is agreed by negotiations between retail operations, buying and merchandising, and finance in December/January and separate negotiations are held between concessions and finance. The plans are analysed in the same way as the first half plans.

(b) Sales plans by branch are agreed by retail operations, concessions, and finance in January.

(c) Cost plans are agreed by branch by retail operations, personnel, and finance in January.

(d) Central cost plans by cost centre are determined by departmental directors and finance in January.

(e) The second half year plan is presented to the divisional, sector and main Boards in February.

10.22 *Monthly performance monitoring*

The performance is monitored at the area and regional levels and finance and costs are monitored at the head office level together with functional directorate staffs. The procedures are considered in the following Paragraphs 10.23 to 10.26.

10.23 *Area performance review*

Area performance reviews are conducted by key participants and budget holders, that is, the area managers together with the management accountants. The review centres on:

(a) actual profit and loss account performance month by month and the cumulative performance for the half year, branch by branch;

(b) a forecast profit and loss account performance for the half year which is prepared for each branch;

(c) a statement of branch forecast performance is compared to plan performance and any actions to be taken agreed.

10.24 *Regional performance review*

Regional performance reviews are conducted by the regional controllers together with the management accountants. The review is based on:

(a) a statement of branch performance consolidated into areas and regions and compared with plan;

(b) a prepared standard report of forecast key ratios compared to plan:

- by branch;
- by area;
- by region.

(c) The key ratios include:

- sales per square foot;
- contribution per square foot;
- sales per employee;
- contribution per employee.

10.25 *Finance review*

Finance reviews are conducted by the retails operations director with the finance director/controller. They review:

(a) significant variations from plan on cumulative and forecast performance;

(b) 'balance to achieve' performance required to achieve divisional targets.

10.26 *Central cost review*

Central cost reviews are conducted by functional directors with the financial controller. The reviews consider:

(a) actual performance in month and cumulatively and forecast divisional performance for the half year compared with plan;

(b) forecast costs for half year compared with plan and needed actions identified.

10.27 *Preparation of monthly finance package*

Monthly finance packages are prepared by corporate finance and submitted to divisional, sector and main boards. The following statements are prepared:

(a) cumulative divisional performance for the half year compared with plan together with explanation of major variances;

(b) detailed sales and margin analysis including stock and mark-down summary and report on stock losses;

(c) detailed analysis of branch and central costs;

(d) detailed analysis of balance sheet, funds flow and capital expenditure.

10.28 *Preparation of board papers*

Board papers are prepared by finance staff for the divisional, sector and main boards.

In the first half these include:

- first half forecast;
- second half plan;
- full year forecast;
- five year plan.

In the second half these include:

- first half actuals;
- second half forecast;
- full year forecast;
- next year's plan;
- five year plan.

10.29 Key elements in the budget

The key elements have both main and subsidiary determinants. Nine key elements are identified and used in preparing budgets.

(1) *Growth in monetary sales* is mainly determined by sales price inflation and volume growth. The subsidiary determinants are market growth which is influenced by demographic changes (particularly in terms of age distribution), increases/decreases in spending power in target markets, and changes in lifestyle of target markets.

(2) *Growth in market share* which is influenced by increases in sales per square foot through competitive advantage, industry restructuring, and higher translation of customer footfall into sales.

(3) *Increases in sales per square foot* are influenced by width and depth of range, image, new entrances and exits, additional square footage through opening new shops, and additional products. A regional analysis may be conducted to identify additional products and square footage.

(4) *Gross margins* are mainly determined by mark-up, mark-down, and stock losses. The subsidiary determinants are cost inflation versus price inflation, changes in product mix (which are important when there is a large disparity in mark-up between different product groups and/or when there is a significant swing in the traditional product mix), exchange rates in relation to imported or exported products, achievement of sales budget, terminal stock levels, inventory trends, and security trends.

The monetary value of mark-down is the most difficult of all variables to be precise about since non-achievement of sales budget results in a higher terminal stock and thus a higher mark-down percentage and amount. Stock management and buying policy are therefore critical. The cost of security has to be balanced against the value of stock losses.

(5) *Concession income* is mainly determined by space allocation, and the rate charged for space (which is usually a percentage of sales plus a service charge). A subsidiary determinant is the desired risk profile.

(6) *Branch payroll costs* are mainly determined by the number and grading of employees in each branch, and the overall level of the pay award. The subsidiary determinants are inflation, industry averages, and legislation (for instance on National Health Insurance).

(7) *Rents* Market rents are determined by group property division. Where a company holds its own property portfolio the balance among short and long leasehold and freehold properties will be critical in determining its short and long term profitability.

(8) *Local authority rates or charges* The main determinant used to be local authority policy but Central Government now exercises a large degree of control.

Subsidiary determinants are the location of shops within a local market and the regional distribution of shops.

(9) *Control costs* The main determinants are warehousing and distribution, systems costs, and the functional organisation structure. Subsidiary determinants are the location and size of warehousing facilities and the regional distribution of shops. Warehousing and distribution are managed within the group by a profit making group division. Systems costs and service levels are negotiated with the separately managed group division.

Further key industry issues are cost of goods inflation, exchange rates, Government policies affecting consumer spending (including taxation), interest rates, consumer credit restrictions, employee legislation and Governmental regional policies.

10.30 Monitoring retailing

The principal issues in monitoring retailing operations are related to sales volumes and prices, stock holdings and stock issues.

An aerospace and defence systems company

10.31 Budget management

The budgetary control system in this company is based on forward plans covering the current financial year and four years forward. As the aerospace industry is not normally subject to sudden changes in demand, the company normally has a good idea of likely demand over the budget periods.

10.32 Budget timetable

An agreed budget preparation timetable is circulated to executives about two-and-a-half months before the date for completing the budget in time for the start of the budget period.

10.33 Tasks and deadlines

A detailed list of tasks with deadlines and those responsible for meeting them is circulated with the timetable. The first deadlines are about three to four weeks after the start of budget preparation. Work is carried out simultaneously on various tasks.

10.34 *Personnel and cost trends*

As a first step, the management accountant and cost accountant discuss with departmental managers:

- listings of indirect personnel employed;
- trends in expenditure.

10.35 *Sales forecasts*

At the same time, marketing services discuss and agree the long-term sales forecast with marketing managers. The forecast is:

- by product code;
- by sales outlet;
- valued at existing selling prices.

10.36 *Sales budget and stock levels*

The sales budget is prepared by the marketing director and discussed with the management accountant for decisions on:

- levels of warehouse stocks;
- production work-in-progress.

10.37 *Materials and labour requirements*

Based on the required demand to meet the sales budget, factory management prepare estimates for:

- material requirements;
- labour skills needed.

10.38 *Development and general engineering*

Development and general engineering is a significant part of the business. A budget for the various engineering skills required is prepared, together with a budget for the development programme.

10.39 *Factory operating budget*

The cost accountant produces a factory operating budget on the basis of:

- gang labour rates;
- number of direct operators required;

- departmental expense budgets.

An assessment of the level of expenditure recoverable from the customer is prepared and the balance is chargeable against profit.

10.40 *Trading budget*

A draft trading budget is prepared by the management accountant and there is then a process of 'fine tuning' the budgeted expenditure.

An assessment of the likely level of inflation is made and applied, as appropriate, to the estimates for:

- labour;
- materials;
- expenses;
- sales.

From these figures, a trading budget is prepared at average values for the budget year.

10.41 *Funds budget*

A funds budget is prepared at the same time covering:

(a) *Fixed Assets*

Scheduling of replacement and additional equipment, the timing of acquisitions and the calculation of depreciation.

(b) *Stocks*

Movement in volume and value by reference to the likely turnover in the following year.

(c) *Trade Debtors*

Volume of sales and success of credit control.

(d) *Trade Creditors*

Volume of purchases and credit available.

(e) *Other debtors/creditors*

Various judgements.

10.42 *Tax, interest and cash flow*

When the trading budget and funds movement is available, the management accountant calculates:

- likely level of interest payable/receivable;
- tax liability;
- net cash movement.

10.43 *Key budget statistics*

The final stage is to prepare a final schedule of key statistics showing:

- total sales;
- trading profit;
- property income;
- interest/finance charges;
- profit after interest;
- inflation adjustment;
- profit after inflation;
- corporation tax;
- profits after tax;
- dividends;
- retained profit;
- increase/decrease in borrowings;
- funds employed.

This format is later used for monitoring, as noted in Paragraph 10.46 below.

10.44 *Headcount*

The personnel information is summarised to show:

- direct factory personnel;
- other personnel.

10.45 *Key budget indicators*

The following ratios are prepared on the basis of the budget statements:

- % trading profit to total sales;
- % trading profit to funds employed excluding property;
- % profit after inflation to funds employed;
- % gross profit to sales;
- % trade debtors to previous quarter sales;

- % stock to annual sales;
- trade creditors as number of weeks;
- % payroll to value added.

10.46 *Budget comparisons*

For comparison, all the budget figures and indicators for the previous three years are shown at one side of the form. At the other side are shown the figures for the current month, the cumulative for the year and the forecast (budget) figure.

10.47 *Standard cost up-date*

About two weeks after the budget has been agreed, this company starts a programme for updating standard costs. The timetable is as follows:

Time from Budget Set	Function	Action by:
Week 1	Establish labour rates	Chief Accountant
Week 2	Establish overhead rates	Chief Accountant
Week 2	Establish material and labour excess levels	Chief Estimator
Week 6	Establish file of major bought out standards	Buying Office
Week 6	Set commodity code uplifts	Buying Office
Week 6	Set sub-contract standards	Buying Office
Week 10	Freeze bill of materials file and amend as necessary for standard cost revision file	Management Services
Week 10	Freeze operations master file and amend as necessary for standard cost revision file.	Management Services
Week 10	Final processing	Management Services
Week 10	Final checking	Chief Estimator
Week 14	Transfer standard cost revision file to annual standard cost file	Management Accountant
Week 14	Process amendments on annual standard cost file	Management Accountant

An international food and drinks group

10.48 An example of published company objectives

The 1984 annual report and accounts of the Cadbury-Schweppes Group gave a summary of the objectives set for their own managers at that time. The objectives cover both business and financial aims and are reproduced in the following paragraphs, 10.49 and 10.50.

10.49 Business objectives

(a) The group will concentrate on its principal business areas of confectionery, soft drinks beverages and food products. The objective is to maximise use of existing assets rather than diversify into unrelated areas.

(b) In confectionery the company holds 5 per cent of the world chocolate market and is ranked fifth largest company. They intend to increase that share and to climb the league of international chocolate companies.

(c) In soft drinks they are currently number three in the market outside the USA but fifth in the world overall. They aim to become the world's leading non-cola carbonated soft drinks company.

(d) The organisation structure is based on product streams to encourage the maximum use of assets on a worldwide basis through product sourcing and effective planning of capital expenditure.

(e) The group aims to build on its strong personnel traditions of its companies by bringing about greater accountability and decentralisation,honest assessment of performance,reward related to their progress as a business and a management style based on openness and participation.

As can be seen, the first three business objectives are concerned with market position of the group and the fourth stresses that the organisation structure is based on product streams. Clearly, the development and marketing of products is an important element, perhaps the most important, in this group's business objectives and strategy.

10.50 Financial objectives

The group states its financial objectives as follows:

(a) Earnings per share:

5 per cent increase per annum in real terms.

(b) *Return on assets:*

25 per cent per annum.

(c) *Gearing:*

ratio of debt to equity to be below 50 per cent.

(d) *Interest cover:*

trading profit to be at least five times greater than interest charges.

(e) *Dividend cover:*

earnings to cover dividends up to three times.

11
Specimen Forms

During its investigations, the working party collected well over two hundred forms from the companies co-operating with CIMA on this guide. All were interesting and the difficult thing was to know what to leave out. The first thought was to reproduce a complete and internally consistent set of forms to illustrate how to cater for all budget needs, but that might place too much emphasis on one industry. In any case, the reader will have to adapt any examples to meet his or her own requirements. So, we have taken forms from several systems to illustrate the main aspects of budgeting. With a little effort and imagination these should be easily adapted to meet most needs.

11.1 Profit and loss account

This shows the profit and loss account for last year (actual 1989), the latest estimate for the current year (1990) and the planned budget for next year (1991). The final two columns display in money and percentage terms the difference between current year estimate and the budget for next year.

11.2 Phased (quarterly) profit and loss account

This shows the expected breakdown of sales volumes, sales revenues and expenses for each quarter of the budget year. The index gives the percentage of each item in each quarter.

11.3 Balance sheet

This shows the balance sheet for last year (actual 1989), the best estimate for the current year (1990) and the planned budget for next year (1991).

11.4 Phased (monthly) balance sheet

This shows a budgeted balance sheet for thirteen months covering the period from September 1990 to September 1991. The budget year starts in October.

11.5 Funds flow statement

This is a statement of the flow of funds for last year (actual 1989), the best estimate for the current year (1990) and the planned budget for next year (1991).

11.6 *Phased (monthly) funds flow statement*

This monthly phased flow of funds statement covers the budget year from October 1990 to September 1991.

11.7 *Phased (monthly) cash and funds flow statement*

This is another statement showing the budgeted cash/funds flow month by month for the calendar year 1990.

11.8 *Capital expenditure summary*

This presents the amounts approved for capital expenditure projects in the current year, 1989/90 (classified by monetary size: under £100m; £100m to £500m; and over $500m). There is a column for approved cost changes and then a column for approvals brought forward from the previous year, 1988/89. These provide the total carry forward to the budget year, 1990/91. The total is then broken down according to whether it will appear as a revenue or a capital item in the budgets.

11.9 *Phased (monthly) capital expenditure summary*

This registers budget capital expenditure month by month for the budget year 1990/91 but gives figures for thirteen calendar months (as in 11.4).

11.10 *Brand profitability analysis*

This registers the brand sales volume, revenues and contribution for last year (actual 1989), the best estimate for the current year (1990) and the planned budget for next year (1991). A separate form is required for each brand.

11.11 *Discretionary marketing expenditure*

This shows the planned discretionary expenditures for a brand for last year (actual 1989), the best estimate for the current year (1990) and the planned budget for next year (1991). A separate form is required for each brand.

11.12 *Brand price analysis*

This details the various components of price for each brand for last year (actual 1989), the best estimate for the current year (1990) and the planned budget for next year (1991).

11.13 Other income and expenditure and exceptional items

This discloses various items of other income and expenditures and exceptional items. The item as forecast in the third forecast of the current year, 1989/90, the change in money and percentage terms and the amount for budget year 1990/91.

11.14 Estimated tax computation

This discloses the items leading to the calculation of tax payable, deferred tax and amounts allowable/disallowable. A reconciliation is shown. Separate forms are completed for current year and plan.

11.15 Phased current liabilities

This lists the external, intra-group and inter-group borrowing, tax and dividends for thirteen calendar months.

11.16 Newspaper product prices

The form outlines advertisement rates and increases in cover prices for previous year (1989), current year (1990) and next year plan (1991).

11.17 Newspaper revenue and cost variance analysis

This shows revenue variance due to price and volume changes comparing current year (1990) to next year budget (1991) in terms of £000's and percentages. Newsprint costs are also analysed.

11.18 Wages, materials and expenses variance

The form shows the above actual costs for the previous year (1989), estimate for current year (1990) and plan for budget year (1991) and the variance (1991 on 1990). A separate form is completed for each department.

11.19 Phased (monthly) employee and payroll costs

This shows the number of employees, direct and indirect, and the associated labour costs for the budget twelve months, October 1990 to September 1991.

11.20 Cost allocation analysis

The form exhibits volumes sold and produced with associated production and service costs charged to profit and loss account for the previous year (1989), estimate for current year (1990 and budget for next year (1991), with cost allocation analysis for year 1991.

11.21 Branch and head office controllable expenses

This shows branch expenses separated between those controllable by the branch and those controlled by head office.

11.22 Phased (monthly) stocks analysis

Reflects various stocks held, by value, the number of weeks, and the debtors in equivalent sales days for September 1990 and each of the budget 12 months from October 1990 to September 1991.

11.23 Analysis of debtors

Exhibits debtors outstanding analysed according to terms of trade (six categories from up to fifteen days up to over four months), prompt payment discounts, and the total analysed between not yet due and total overdue. There is a time analysis of the overdue balances. Both actual and budget days sales equivalents are shown.

11.24 Key costs and productivity ratios

Gives key indicators for actual previous year, current year estimate and next year budget.

11.25 Downside sensitivity analysis

Illustrates the main budget items with a calculation of the propensity to change if activity falls.

11.26 Transfer price analysis

This shows purchases and sales volumes and transfer prices. For sales, the gross contribution and net profit and a contribution ratio is also shown for each product by profit centre.

11.27 Profit and loss control statement

The items on lines 1 to 21 indicate the sales volumes and profit and loss account items from sales revenues through to profit before tax. Against each line, columns 1 and 2 show the current month actual and variance from budget. Columns 3 and 4 depict cumulative actual and budget variance for the year to date. Column 5 the cumulative amount for the corresponding period in the last year, and column 6 the half year estimate. Columns 7 and 8 show the estimate for the full year and the expected variance from budget.

11.28 Variance summary explanations and actions

This form is used to portray the explanations for the cost, contribution and profit variances and the actions taken. Lines 300 to 310 reconcile the budget to actual operating profits with column 1 showing the figures for the month and column 2, cumulative data for the year to date. Lines 311 to 318 analyse the variance between volume and mix.

Columns 3 and 4 are used for the explanations of variances and statements of actions taken.

11.29 Forecast variance summary

The lines are the same as in Form 11.28, but the first column shows actuals for year to date, columns 2 and 3 show the forecasts for the rest of the year and for the full year. Columns 4 and 5 are provided for explanations and actions to be taken.

11.30 Market share analysis

Reveals the moving annual total of total market, sector and market share, monthly, for each product over one year.

11.31 Net debt analysis

Registers the various components of external and internal group debt cumulative for the year to date, an estimate of the balance expected at year end, September, and an estimate of the balance at end of fifteen months. Monthly estimates for the next six months are given in columns 4 to 9.

Form 11.1 Profit and Loss Account

OPERATING GROUP .... CURRENCY ....
PROFIT CENTRE NAME/CODE ....

	LINE	1988/89 ACTUAL	1989/90 BUDGET	1989/90 LATEST ESTIMATE	%	1990/91 BUDGET OUTLINE	%	1990/91 ANNUAL BUDGET	%	CHANGE FROM BUDGET OUTLINE %
VOLUMES (UNITS.......)	1									
SALES REVENUE	2									
Less Duty	3									
SALES EXCLUDING DUTY	4									
Other Variable Costs	5									
GROSS CONTRIBUTION	6									
Discretionary Marketing	7									
MARKETING CONTRIBUTION	8									
OPERATING COSTS Manufacturing	9									
Engineering	10									
Distribution	11									
Marketing - Fixed	12									
Sales Force	13									
Administration	14									
TOTAL OPERATING COSTS	15									
OPERATING PROFIT	16									
Other Income/(Costs)	17									
TRADING PROFIT	18									
Interest Cost/(Income)	19									
PROFIT BEFORE TAX	20									

Form 11.2 Phased (Quarterly) Profit and Loss Account

OPERATING GROUP ....   CURRENCY ....

PROFIT CENTRE NAME/CODE ....

	LINE	QUARTER 1	QUARTER 2	HALF YEAR	QUARTER 3	QUARTER 4	FULL YEAR
VOLUME - UNITS							
- LATEST EST 1989/90	1						
- BUDGET 1990/91	2						
BUDGET PHASING INDEX	3						100
SALES REVENUE (EXCLUDING DUTY)							
- LATEST EST 1989/90	4						
- BUDGET 1990/91	5						
BUDGET PHASING INDEX	6						100
DISCRETIONARY MARKETING							
- LATEST EST 1989/90	7						
- BUDGET 1990/91	8						
BUDGET PHASING INDEX	9						100
OPERATING COSTS (Exc Disc Marketing)							
- LATEST EST 1989/90	10						
- BUDGET 1990/91	11						
BUDGET PHASING INDEX	12						100
OPERATING PROFIT							
- LATEST EST 1989/90	13						
- BUDGET 1990/91	14						
BUDGET PHASING INDEX	15						100

Form 11.3 Balance Sheet

OPERATIONAL PLAN 1991

CENTRE

BALANCE SHEET
£000

	RECONCILIATION	1989 ACTUAL	1990 LATEST ESTIMATE	1991 PLAN
SHARE CAPITAL	—			
SUBORDINATED LOAN STOCK/PAID IN CAPITAL	—			
RESERVES	1			
RETAINED PROFITS	2			
SHAREHOLDERS' FUNDS				
UK GOVERNMENT GRANTS	3			
DEFERRED TAXATION	4			
LONG TERM DEBT — Non current portion	—			
LOAN ACCOUNT	5			
UK GROUP TAX RELIEF:				
(Receivable)/Payable — current year	—			
— earlier years	—			
CURRENT TAX — on current year's profits	—			
— on earlier year's profits	—			
BANK OVERDRAFTS AND SHORT-TERM LOANS	—			
DIVIDENDS PAYABLE/(GROUP DIVIDENDS RECEIVABLE)				
FIXED ASSETS	6			
PUBLISHING RIGHTS	7			
GOODWILL	8			
INVESTMENTS	9			
INTEREST IN SUBSIDIARIES	10			
RECONCILIATION ACCOUNT				
CURRENT ASSETS/(LIABILITIES):				
Stock				
Debtors, prepayments, deposits & advances etc	—			
Creditors, accruals and deferred revenue etc				
(including Recon A/c's)	11	( )	( )	( )
MANAGED ASSETS				
CASH AND BANK BALANCES, BANK TERM DEPOSITS,				
SHORT-TERM INVESTMENTS	—			

Form 11.4 Phased (Monthly) Balance Sheet

OPERATING GROUP .... PERIOD 1990/91 PHASED BUDGET

PROFIT CENTRE NAME/CODE ....

Currency ....

	LINE	SEPT 90	OCT 90	NOV 90	DEC 90	JAN 91	FEB 91	MAR 91	APR 91	MAY 91	JUN 91	JUL 91	AUG 91	SEPT 91
GOODWILL	1													
TANGIBLE ASSETS: Land and Buildings	2													
Plant and machinery	3													
INVESTMENTS: Trade	4													
Subsidiaries	5													
Associates	6													
TOTAL NON CURRENT ASSETS	7													
CURRENT ASSETS: Stock	8													
External Debtors	9													
Group Debtors	10													
Cash and deposits	11													
	12													
CURRENT LIABILITIES: Ext. creditors	13													
Group creditors	14													
Overdrafts & short term borrowings	15													
Current taxation	16													
Dividends	17													
Provisions	18													
	19													
NET CURRENT ASSETS	20													
TOTAL EMPLOYMENT OF CAPITAL	21													
TOTAL SHAREHOLDERS' FUNDS	22													
DEFERRED TAX	23													
LOANS: External	24													
Inter/Intra Group Net	25													
TOTAL CAPITAL EMPLOYED	26													

Form 11.5 Funds Flow Statement

OPERATING GROUP .... CURRENCY ....
PROFIT CENTRE NAME/CODE ....

	LINE	1989/90 ACTUAL	1990/91 BUDGET	1990/91 LATEST ESTIMATE	1991/92 BUDGET OUTLINE	1991/92 ANNUAL BUDGET	CHANGE FROM BUDGET OUTLINE
PROFIT BEFORE TAX	1						
ADD BACK: Depreciation	2						
Provisions	3						
Other/Non Cash Items	4						
FUNDS GENERATED FROM OPERATIONS	5						
Changes in Working Capital:							
Stocks (increase)/decrease	6						
External Debtors (increase)/decrease	7						
External Creditors increase/(decrease)	8						
Change in Inter/Intra Group Trade A/Cs	9						
Change in Inter/Intra Group Non-Trade	10						
NET CHANGE IN WORKING CAPITAL	11						
FIXED ASSETS							
— (Additions)	12						
— Disposals	13						
— NET FIXED ASSETS	14						
GROUP AND TRADE INVESTMENTS	15						
TOTAL OUTFLOW OF FUNDS	16						
NET OPERATING FUNDS FLOW	17						

Form 11.6 Phased (Monthly) Funds Flow Statement

OPERATING GROUP .... PERIOD 1990/91 ....
PROFIT CENTRE NAME/CODE ....

	LINE	OCT 90	NOV 90	DEC 90	JAN 91	FEB 91	MAR 91	APR 91	MAY 91	JUN 91	JUL 91	AUG 91	SEPT 91	TOTAL
PROFIT Before Tax	1													
Add Back: Depreciation	2													
Provisions	3													
Other non cash items	4													
FUNDS GENERATED FROM OPERATION	5													
Changes in working capital:														
Stock (increase)/decrease	6													
External debtors (incr)/decr	7													
External creditors incr/(decr)	8													
Change in group debtors/creditors	9													
NET CHANGE IN WORKING CAPITAL	10													
Changes in fixed assets:														
Tangible Assets — (Additions)	11													
— Disposals	12													
Investments — (Additions)	13													
— Disposals	14													
NET CHANGE IN FIXED ASSETS	15													
TOTAL OUTFLOW OF FUNDS	16													
NET OPERATING FUNDS FLOW	17													

Form 11.7 Phased (Monthly) Cash and Funds Flow Statement

OPERATIONAL PLAN 1990

CENTRE _____

PHASED CASH FLOW (£'000)

	January	February	March	April	May	June	July	August	September	October	November	December	TOTAL
TURNOVER Group													
Outside													
Total													
PROFIT AND LOSS ACCOUNT													
Pre-tax Profit/(Loss)													
Depreciation (before Gov Grant Cr.)													
Amortisation of Goodwill/PR													
Capital Loss/(Profit)													
Other Non Cash Movements (Specify):													
Sub Total													
BALANCE SHEET													
Interest Accrual													
Loan Account Movements													
Interest on Loan Account													
Cash (Remitted)/Received													
Tax paid													
Group Relief Payments/(Receipts)													
Working Capital Movements													
(Inc)/Dec in Stock													
(Inc)/Dec in Advert Debtors													
(Inc)/Dec in News Debtors													
(Inc)/Dec in Other Debtors													
(Inc)/Dec in Prepayments													
Movement in Recon A/c													
Inc/(Dec) in Creditors (Including other Recon A/c's)													
Capital Receipts — Fixed Assets													
Capital Receipts — Other (Specify)													
Capital Grants — Receipts													
— (Credited to P & L)													
Group Relief Receipts													
Taxation Repayments													
Other Receipts (Specify):													
TOTAL FUNDS GENERATED													
Capital Expenditure													
Inter Group Transfer of Asset													
Purchase of Investments													
Dividends Paid													
Group Relief Payments													
Taxation Payments													
Other Payments (Specify):													
TOTAL FUNDS UTILISED													
Net Surplus/(Deficit)													
Opening Balance (Overdraft)													
Closing Balance (Overdraft)													
Days Outstanding:													
Adverts													
Newsagents													

Form 11.8 Capital Expenditure Summary

BUDGET 1990/91
CAPITAL EXPENDITURE — SUMMARY

	Project Initiations Approved for 1989/90			New Projects /Cost Changes Since Approval £000	Brought Forward From 1988/89 (inc. Rev) £000	Carry Forward To 1990/91 (inc. Rev) £000	Expenditure Budget 1990/91	
	Over m£500 Each £000	m£100 to m£500 Each £000	Under m£100 Each £000				Revenue Element £000	Capital Element £000
Retail Division								
— Operations								
— Projects								
— Fitting Out Costs								
Distribution Division								
Production								
Central Departments								
Private Vehicles								
Branch Development Division (excluding New Branches & Extensions)								
TOTAL								
New Branches & Extensions (including interest on Loan)								
Site Purchases								
TOTAL CAPITAL EXPENDITURE 1990/91								
Oncost								
TOTAL GROSS CAPITAL EXPENDITURE								
Site — Sales								
NET CAPITAL EXPENDITURE 1990/91								

Form 11.9 Phased (Monthly) Capital Expenditure Summary

BUDGET 1990/91
CAPITAL EXPENDITURE — PHASING

BUDGET 1990/91 £000

	1	2	3	4	5	6	7	8	9	10	11	12	13	TOTAL
Retail Division														
- Operations														
- Projects														
- Fitting Out Costs														
Distribution Division														
Production														
Central Departments														
Private Vehicles														
Branch Development (Excluding new Branches and Extensions)														
TOTAL														
New Branches & Extensions (Including Interest on Loan)														
Sites — Purchases														
TOTAL CAPITAL EXPENDITURE 1990/91														
Oncost														
TOTAL GROSS CAPITAL EXPENDITURE 1990/91														
Sites — Sales														
NET CAPITAL EXPENDITURE 1990/91														

Form 11.10 Brand Profitability Analysis

OPERATING GROUP .... CURRENCY ....
PROFIT CENTRE NAME/CODE ....
BRAND ....

	1988/89 ACTUAL	1989/90 BUDGET	1989/90 LATEST ESTIMATE	%	1990/91 BUDGET OUTLINE	%	1990/91 ANNUAL BUDGET	%	CHANGE FROM BUDGET OUTLINE %
1. VOLUME									
2. GROSS SALES REVENUE (Ex Duty) — per bb/hl — total									
DISCOUNTS & REBATES — per bb/hl — total									
NET SALES REVENUE — per bb/hl — total									
3. GROSS CONTRIBUTION — per bb/hl — total									
4. % GROSS CONTRIBUTION									
5. DISCRETIONARY MARKETING — per bb/hl — total — % of sales revenue									
6. MARKETING CONTRIBUTION — per bb/hl — total — % of sales revenue									

Form 11.11 Discretionary Marketing Expenditure

OPERATING GROUP .... CURRENCY ....
PROFIT CENTRE NAME/CODE ....
BRAND ....

	LINE	1988/89 ACTUAL	1989/90 BUDGET	1989/90 LATEST ESTIMATE	%	1990/91 ANNUAL BUDGET	%	LEAD TIME	AND	COMMENTS
MEDIA SPACE										
TV	1									
RADIO	2									
CINEMA	3									
PRESS	4									
POSTERS	5									
	6									
MEDIA PRODUCTION										
TV	7									
RADIO	8									
CINEMA	9									
PRESS	10									
POSTERS	11									
	12									
POINT OF SALE	13									
PROMOTIONS CONSUMER ON	14									
CONSUMER OFF	15									
TRADE	16									
SPONSORSHIPS	17									
PUBLIC RELATIONS	18									
MARKET RESEARCH	19									
PRODUCT DEVELOPMENT	20									
OTHER	21									
	22									
TOTAL DISCRETIONARY MARKETING	23									

Form 11.12 Brand Price Analysis

OPERATING GROUP .... CURRENCY ....
PROFIT CENTRE NAME/CODE ....

PER HL/BBL	RETAIL SELLING PRICE	SALES TAX	NET RSP	RETAIL MARGIN	W/SALE MARGIN	GROSS PRICE	DISCOUNTS/ REBATES	DUTY	NET SELLING PRICE
Brand:									
1988/89 Actual									
1989/90 Lat.Est.									
1990/91 Budget									
Brand:									
1988/89 Actual									
1989/90 Lat.Est.									
1990/91 Budget									
Brand:									
1988/89 Actual									
1989/90 Lat.Est.									
1990/91 Budget									
Brand:									
1988/89 Actual									
1989/90 Lat.Est.									
1990/91 Budget									

Form 11.13 Other Income and Expenditure and Exceptional Items

	3rd Profits Forecast 1989/90	CHANGE IN COST		Budget 1990/91
		£000	% Change	£000
OTHER INCOME & EXPENDITURE				
Profit on Redemption of Debentures				
Other Oncost recovery				
Previous Year's Adjustments				
Suppliers Balances				
VAT Suspense				
HMP Management Charge				
Branch computing project				
XYZ Provision				
Manufacturers Coupon Handling Allowance				
N.I. Surcharge Rebate				
TOTAL				
EXCEPTIONAL ITEMS				
Sale & Leaseback Profits				
Profit on sale of property				
Distribution Contingency				
Period 14 depreciation, write back				
Liabilities Provision				
TOTAL				
CAPITALISATION OF INTEREST				

Form 11.14 Estimated Tax Computation

OPERATIONAL PLAN 1990
CENTRE _____

11.14 Estimated tax computation
(Complete Separate Computations for 1989 and 1990)

	Tax Payable £000 (a)	Deferred Tax £000 (b)	Allowable/ (Disallowable) £000 (d)
Pre-Tax Profit			
Add: Amotrisation of Goodwill/PR			
Depreciation — gross			
Deduct: Government Grants credited to P & L			
Capital Allowances:			
Initial/First Year			
Writing Down			
Balancing			
Add/Deduct: Other timing differences (if material)			
Non-Taxable items included in Pre-Tax Profit (If material)			
Totals			

Reconciliation	£000	* Rate %	£000
(a) Tax Payable		at %	
(b) Movement in Deferred Tax		at %	
(c) Subtotal — Taxation			
(d) Disallowable		at %	(for reconciliation only)
Pre-Tax Profits		at %	

* 1989 = 46.25%, 1990 = 41.25%

Form 11.15 Phased Current Liabilities

OPERATING GROUP .... PERIOD ....
PROFIT CENTRE NAME/CODE ....

	LINE	SEPT 90	OCT 90	NOV 90	DEC 90	JAN 91	FEB 91	MAR 91	APR 91	MAY 91	JUN 91	JUL 91	AUG 91	SEPT 91
OVERDRAFTS & SHORT TERM BORROWING														
External	1													
Inter group	2													
Intra group	3													
TOTAL	4													
CURRENT TAXATION														
External	5													
Inter group	6													
Intra group	7													
TOTAL	8													
DIVIDENDS														
External	9													
Inter group	10													
Intra group	11													
TOTAL	12													
DEBTORS DAYS	13													

Form 11.16 Newspaper Product Prices

OPERATIONAL PLAN 1991
CENTRE ....

Newspaper Advertisement Rates and Cover Price Increases

	1989		1990		1991		Extra Revenue in Plan Year £000	Extra Revenue in Full Year £000
	Date of Increase	Increase %	Date of Increase	Increase %	Date of Proposed Increase	Increase %		
Advertisement Rates:								
Display								
Classified — Sits Vac								
— Property								
— Motors								
— Other								
Cover Prices:		from p. to p.		from p. to p.		from p. to p.		
Mornings								
Evenings								
Saturday Sports								
Sunday/Weekly								

Form 11.17 Newspaper Revenue and Cost Variance Analysis

OPERATIONAL PLAN 1991

CENTRE _____

11.17 Newspaper Revenue and Cost Variance analysis

	Variance 91/90 Est £000	Amount due to price £000	Amount due to volume £000	Variance 91/90 Est %	Due to Price %	Due to Volume %
Advertisement Revenue						
Main Edition						
National — London — Provincial						
Local						
Classified — Sits. Vacant — Property — Motors — Others						
Group						
Total Main Edition						
Zoned Edition						
TMC'S						
Supplements						
Total Advertising						
Newspaper Sales Revenue						
Other Revenue						
Total Revenue						
Newsprint Cost						

Form 11.18 Wages, Materials and Expenses Variance

OPERATIONAL PLAN 1991

CENTRE ....

DEPARTMENT ....   DEPARTMENTAL COSTS

	1989 Actual £	1990 Estimate £	1991 Plan £	1991 Variance £
A. WAGES				
Wages and Salaries				
Bonus				
Overtime				
Social Security				
TOTAL (A)				

STAFFING

	1989	1990	1991			Explanation of variant £
				1990 Awards		
				1991 National Awards		
				1991 Local Agreements		
				1991 Salary Reviews		
				Staffing Levels		
				Overtime		
				Bonus		
Plan Total				Vacancies		
Vacancies				Other		
Payroll Total				E N I	Variance as above	

B.   MATERIALS AND EXPENSES
     (Nominal Ledger A/cs)

	£	£	£	£
TOTAL (B)				
DEPARTMENTAL TOTAL (A + B)				

Form 11.19 Phased (Monthly) Employee and Payroll Costs

OPERATING GROUP .... PERIOD 1990/91 PHASED BUDGET

PROFIT CENTRE NAME/CODE ....

	Line	OCT 90	NOV 90	DEC 90	JAN 91	FEB 91	MAR 91	APR 91	MAY 91	JUN 91	JUL 91	AUG 91	SEPT 91	TOTAL
NUMBER OF EMPLOYEES														
Direct Labour (Other Var Costs)	1													
Indirect Labour (Manufacturing)	2													
Engineering	3													
Distribution	4													
Marketing	5													
Sales Force	6													
Administration	7													
Total Number of Employees	8													
PAYROLL COSTS (CURRENCY ....)														
Direct Labour (Other Var Costs)	9													
Indirect Labour (Manufacturing)	10													
Engineering	11													
Distribution	12													
Marketing	13													
Sales Force	14													
Administration	15													
TOTAL PAYROLL COSTS	16													

Form 11.20 Cost Allocation Analysis

OPERATING GROUP

PROFIT CENTRE NAME/CODE

CURRENCY

	LINE	1989 ACTUAL	TOTAL COST 1990 LATEST EST	1991 ANN. BUDGET	DUTY	VARIABLE COSTS	MANUFACTURING	ENGINEERING	DISTRIBUTION
					\\\\\\\\	\\\\\\\\	\\\\\\\\	\\\\\\\\	\\\\\\\\
VOLUME SOLD	1								
VOLUME BREWED	2				\\\\\\\\	\\\\\\\\	\\\\\\\\	\\\\\\\\	\\\\\\\\
BREWING									
Pale Malt	3								
Roast Materials	4								
Hops/Extract	5								
Sundry Mats	6								
CMB, GBS, MF	7								
Finings	8								
Labour	9								
Beer Purchased	10								
Excise Duty	11								
Depreciation	12								
COST OF PROD'N	13								
(RE CHARGES)	14								
CHARGED TO P & L	15								
SERVICES									
Water/Effluent	16								
Oil	17								
Electricity	18								
Labour - Own	19								
Subcontracted	20								
Depreciation	21								
Other Costs	22								
COST OF SERVICES	23								
(RE CHARGES)	24								
CHARGED TO P & L	24								

COST ALLOCATION ANALYSIS 1990/91

Form 11.21 Branch and Head Office Controllable Expenses

BUDGET 1990/91

| | 3rd Profit Forecast 1989/90 | | CHANGE IN COST | | | | BUDGET 1990/91 | | |
| | | | At Constant Price | | Due to Inflation | | | | |
	£000	% of Sales	£000	% Change	£000	% Change	Inflated £000	% of Sales	Total % Change
WAGES & SALARIES									
WAGES & SALARIES									
BRANCH EXPENSES									
Sundry Manpower									
Utilities									
Wrapping Materials									
Hygiene									
Opening Orders									
Cons. Materials									
Equipment									
Catering Food Sub.									
Communications									
Sundry Expenses									
TOTAL BRANCH CONTROLLED									
Rent									
Rates & Service Charges									
Depreciation									
Branch Engineering — Reg. Maint.									
— Jobs									
— SLC Projects									
Equipment & Sundries									
Point of Sale Projects									
XYZ Project									
Cash Collection									
In-store Advertising									
Disturbance & Removal									
TOTAL H.O. CONTROLLED									
Credits									
NET TOTAL H.O. CONTROLLED									
TOTAL BRANCH EXPENSES									

Form 11.22 Phased (Monthly) Stocks Analysis

OPERATING GROUP .... PERIOD ....
PROFIT CENTRE NAME/CODE ....

	LINE	SEPT 90	OCT 90	NOV 90	DEC 90	JAN 91	FEB 91	MAR 91	APR 91	MAY 91	JUN 91	JUL 91	AUG 91	SEPT 91
VALUES														
CMB	1													
Other raw materials	2													
Packaging	3													
Finished products	4													
Engineering spares	5													
Other stocks	6													
TOTAL STOCK VALUES	7													
NO. OF WEEKS														
CMB	8													
Other raw materials	9													
Packaging	10													
Finished products	11													
Engineering spares	12													
Other stocks	13													
TOTAL (Average)	14													
Debtors – Equ. Days Sales	15													

Form 11.23 Analysis of Debtors

OPERATING GROUP
PROFIT CENTRE NAME/CODE

PERIOD

ANALYSIS OF DEBTORS

TERMS OF TRADE	LINE	PROMPT PAYMENT DISCOUNT	Total	Not yet due	Total overdue	ANALYSIS OF OVERDUE BALANCES (MONTH OVERDUE)				
						0 - 1	1 - 2	2 - 3	3 - 4	Over 4
Up to 15 days	1									
16 days to 1 month	2									
1 month to 2 months	3									
2 months to 3 months	4									
3 months to 4 months	5									
Over 4 months	6									
TOTAL	7									

	LINE	MONTH END BALANCE
EQUIVALENT DAYS SALES — ACTUAL	8	
EQUIVALENT DAYS SALES — BUDGET	9	

COMMENTS

Form 11.24 Key Costs and Productivity Ratios

PRODUCTION PLANT ....

CURRENCY ....

	1989 ACTUAL	1990 LATEST ESTIMATE	1991 BUDGET
PACKAGING			
KEGGING			
Waste (%)			
Efficiency (%)			
Keg Turnround at peak			
— home (wks)			
— export 1 (")			
— export 2 (")			
Personnel			
Overtime (%)			
Sick/Absent (%)			
Productivity (hls/man year)			
Labour cost (cost/hl)			
BOTTLING			
Waste (%)			
Efficiency (%)			
CANNING			
Waste (%)			
Efficiency (%)			
BOTTLING & CANNING			
Personnel			
Overtime (%)			
Sick/Absent (%)			
Productivity (hls/man year)			
Labour cost (cost/hl)			

	hls	Cost/ hl,km	hls	Cost/ hl,km	hls	Cost/ hl,km
DISTRIBUTION						
Primary — own fleet						
— contract						
Secondary — own fleet						
— contract						
Personnel						
Overtime (%)						
Sick/Absent (%)						

Form 11.25 Downside Sensitivity Analysis

OPERATING GROUP .... CURRENCY ....

PROFIT CENTRE NAME/CODE ....

	LINE	1991 ANNUAL BUDGET	SENSITIVITY	%	EXPLANATIONS
VOLUMES (UNITS)	1				
SALES REVENUE	2				
Less Duty	3				
SALES EXCLUDING DUTY	4				
Other Variable Costs	5				
GROSS CONTRIBUTION	6				
Discretionary Marketing	7				
MARKETING CONTRIBUTION	8				
OPERATING COSTS					
Manufacturing	9				
Engineering	10				
Distribution	11				
Marketing - fixed	12				
Sales Force	13				
Administration	14				
TOTAL OPERATING COSTS	15				
OPERATING PROFIT	16				
Other Income/(Costs)	17				
TRADING PROFIT	18				
Interest Cost/(Income)	19				
PROFIT BEFORE TAX	20				

Form 11.26 Transfer Price Analysis

OPERATING GROUP .... PERIOD ....

PROFIT CENTRE NAME/CODE ....

PROFIT CENTRE BY PRODUCT	LINE	PURCHASES		SALES				
		VOLUMES	TRANSFER PRICE	VOLUMES	TRANSFER PRICE	GROSS CONTRIBUTION	NET PROFIT	CONTRIBUTION PER HL/BBL
	1							
	2							
	3							
	4							
	5							
	6							
	7							
	8							

Form 11.27 Profit and Loss Control Statement

OPERATING GROUP .... PERIOD ....

PROFIT CENTRE NAME/CODE ....

COLUMN	LINE	MONTH Actual	MONTH Variance vs Budget	YEAR TO DATE Actual	YEAR TO DATE Variance vs Budget	LAST YEAR TO DATE	HALF YEAR ESTIMATE	FULL YEAR Estimate	FULL YEAR Variance vs Budget
		1	2	3	4	5	6	7	8
SALES VOLUME	1								
SALES REVENUE	2								
Less Duty	3								
SALES EXCLUDING DUTY	4								
OTHER VARIABLE COSTS	5								
GROSS CONTRIBUTION	6								
Discretionary Marketing	7								
MARKETING CONTRIBUTION	8								
OPERATING COSTS									
Manufacturing	9								
Engineering	10								
Distribution	11								
Marketing - fixed	12								
Sales Force	13								
Administration	14								
Total Operating Costs	16								
OPERATING PROFIT	17								
Other Income/(Costs)	18								
TRADING PROFITS	19								
Interest Income/(Cost)	20								
PROFIT BEFORE TAX	21								

Form 11.28 Variance Summary — Explanations and Actions

OPERATING GROUP .... PERIOD ....

PROFIT CENTRE NAME/CODE ....

SUMMARY	Line	MONTH 1	YEAR TO DATE 2	EXPLANATION OF VARIANCES 3	ACTION TAKEN 4
COLUMN					
BUDGET OPERATING PROFIT	300				
TOTAL GROSS CONTRIBUTION VARIANCE	302				
TOTAL OPERATING COSTS VARIANCES	304				
ACTUAL OPERATING PROFIT	310				

GROSS CONTRIBUTION VARIANCE

(1) VOLUME VARIANCE:

	Line				
Sales	311				
Duty	312				
Other variable cost	313				
TOTAL	314				

(2) MIX VARIANCE:

	Line				
Sales	315				
Duty	316				
Other variable cost	317				
TOTAL	318				

Form 11.29 Forecast Variance Summary

OPERATING GROUP .... PERIOD ....

PROFIT CENTRE NAME/CODE ....

ACTUAL YEAR TO DATE 1	SUMMARY	Line	REST OF YEAR 2	FULL YEAR 3	EXPLANATION OF FORECAST VARIANCE 4	ACTION TO BE TAKEN 5
	BUDGET OPERATING PROFIT	400				
	TOTAL GROSS CONTRIBUTION VARIANCE	402				
	TOTAL OPERATING COST VARIANCES	404				
	ACTUAL/ESTIMATED OPERATING PROFIT	410				

GROSS CONTRIBUTION VARIANCE

		Line				
(1)	VOLUME VARIANCE					
	Sales	411				
	Duty	412				
	Other variable cost	413				
	TOTAL	414				
(2)	MIX VARIANCE					
	Sales	415				
	Duty	416				
	Other variable cost	417				
	TOTAL	418				

Form 11.30 Market Share Analysis

OPERATING GROUP .... PERIOD ....

PROFIT CENTRE NAME/CODE ....

MARKET/UNITS ....

MOVING ANNUAL TOTALS

	OCT	NOV	DEC	JAN	FEB	MAR	APR	MAY	JUN	JUL	AUG	SEP
TOTAL .... MARKET												

PRODUCT

	OCT	NOV	DEC	JAN	FEB	MAR	APR	MAY	JUN	JUL	AUG	SEP
MARKET												
SECTOR SHARE %												
AGS MARKET SHARE %												
MARKET												
SECTOR SHARE %												
AGS MARKET SHARE %												
MARKET												
SECTOR SHARE %												
AGS MARKET SHARE %												
MARKET												
SECTOR SHARE %												
AGS MARKET SHARE %												
MARKET												
SECTOR SHARE %												
AGS MARKET SHARE %												

Form 11.31 Net Debt Analysis

OPERATING .... PERIOD ....

PROFIT CENTRE NAME .... PROFIT CENTRE CODE ....

TREASURY CENTRE ....

CURRENCY ....

Columns	LINE	YEAR TO DATE BALANCE	ESTIMATE OF BALANCE AT SEPTEMBER	ESTIMATE OF BALANCE AT END OF 15 MONTHS	ESTIMATE FOR FORWARD MONTHS 1 - 6					
		1	2	3	4	5	6	7	8	9
EXTERNAL										
Deposits	1									
Cash	2									
(Medium and Long Term Loans)	3									
(Specials)	4									
(Overdrafts and Short Term Borrowings)	5									
NET EXTERNAL	6									
INTERNAL										
Net Loans Within Group	7									
Net Loans Across Group (excluding UK)	8									
Net Loans Across Group (with UK)	9									
NET INTERNAL	10									
NET DEBT AT END OF PERIOD	11									

Bibliography

Arnold, E., 'Budgeting: The Modelling Approach' *Management Accounting* December 1986.

Arnold, E., 'Delegating Budgetary Responsibility' *Public Finance and Accountancy*, 23 January 1987.

Baker, W. M. and Huang, P. 'Group Technology and The Cost Accounting System' *Industrial Management*, May/June 1986.

Beresford Dew, Gee, R. and K. P., *Management Control and Information*, MacMillan, London, 1973.

Bishop, E. B., 'Budgetary Controls and Corporate Plans' *Accountancy Age*, 18 June 1971.

Bryant, J. W. (ed)., *Financial Modelling in Corporate Management*, John Wiley and Sons, Chichester, 1982.

Cocker, M., 'Financial Management and Just-in-Time', *Management Accounting*, March 1989.

Cook, I., Burnett, A. M. and Gordon, P. N., 'CMP and Managing Indirect Costs in the Eighties', *Journal of Cost Management for Manufacturing Industry*, Spring 1988.

Coulthurst, N. J., 'The New Factory', *Management Accounting* (three articles), March, April and May 1989.

Cowe, R. (ed)., *Handbook of Management Accounting*, Gower Publishing Co. Ltd. (in association with CIMA), 1988, 2nd Edn.

Hill, G., 'Physical Distribution' in Cowe, *Handbook of Management Accounting*.

Hiromoto, T., 'Another Hidden Edge – Japanese Management Accounting', *Harvard Business Review*, July-August 1988.

Hofestede, G. H., *The Game of Budget Control*, Tavistock, London, 1968.

Hyndman, N., 'It is time to spread zero-base budgeting gospel', *Accountancy Age*, 25 February 1982.

Kaplan, R. S., 'Yesterday's Accounting Undermines Production' *Harvard Business Review*, July-August 1984.

Maskell, B., 'Performance Measurement for World Class Manufacturing', *Management Accounting* (four articles), May, June, July/August, and September 1989.

Schonberger, R., *World Class Manufacturing*, 1986.

Simmonds, K., 'Strategic Management Accounting' in Cowe, *Handbook of Management Accounting*.

Wilson, R., 'Marketing and the Management Accountant' in Cowe, *Handbook of Management Accounting*.

INDEX

absenteeism 111
accountability 9
accounting policies 12
accounts classification 20
actual plus budget 96
actual plus forecast 96
actual spending comparison 95
administration
   of budgetary process 5-20
   profit and loss 30-31
administrative staff 68
advanced manufacturing technology
   103-104
advertising allocations 49
aerospace and defence systems
   company 130-134
after-tax earnings 24
allowances and benefits 68
area performance review 127
Arnold, Eric 13, 64
asset
   budgeting 73-77
   targets 40-41
   turnover rate 25
assets
   coming on stream 76
   current 32-33, 85
   definition 74
   fixed 31-32, 75-76, 83-84, 132
   new 76-77
   used (value) 40-41
associates, investment in 32
average fixed cost 66-67

balance sheet 31-36, 85, 137
before-tax earnings 24
behavioural traits 42
benefits 68-69
board 26, 114, 128
borrowings 34, 84
bottom up approach 121
branch expenses 129, 140
brand
   leadership 49
   prices 56, 138
   profitability 41, 138
   volume/market share by 47, 56
budget
   audit 95
   centres 9-10, 94
   comparisons 10, 97, 134
   definition 1
   factors 8-9, 12

   guidelines 26-27, 121-122
   management 130
   manual 19-20
   period 10-11, 124
   preparation 14, 15
   purposes 7
   review 6, 100
   setting 6
   statements 1
   structure 7
budget timetable 14, 16
   aerospace company 130
   for group 18-19, 117-119
   supermarket chain 122-3
budgetary control 1
budgetary process (administration)
   5-20
   computer-integrated
      manufacture and 105
   for sales force 69-70
   special problems 103-116
   systems/stages 5-6
   see also asset budgeting;
      company budgeting
      procedures
budgets
   continuous 11-12
   expenditure control 90
   factory operating 131-132
   financial objectives 21-36
   flexible 10, 12, 95, 97
   funds 132
   forecasts 96, 121
   group 16-19, 117-119
   master 6, 12, 14, 114
   operating 12
   rolling 11-12, 95
   service department 12, 99
   strategic 2
   for subsidiaries 17
   trading 132
Burnett, A.M. 60, 112, 115
business level planning 22
business objectives 7-8, 23-24, 38,
   135
business strategy 7, 90
business year 11

Cadbury-Schweppes Group 135
calendarisation 11
cannibalisation 53
capital
   budgeting 73

expenditure budgeting 2
expenditure summary 138
see also working capital
cash 33, 82, 86, 132-133, 138
central cost review 128
centralisation 13
closed systems 61
Cocker, M. 107
collection periods 25
committed fixed costs 66
company 39, 41-42, 49
company budgeting procedures
  aerospace and defence systems
  130-134
  fashion chain 124-130
  food and drinks company
  135-136
  newspaper group 117-121
  supermarket chain 121-124
competition 17, 51-52
completion time 16
component fixed cost 65
components 99
computer-aided design 104
computer-aided manufacture 104
computer-integrated manufacture
  105
concession income 129
consultants 46
consumer trends 49
contingency funds 14
continuous budgets 11-12
contribution analysis 57
control
  costs 130
  funds flow 91
  labour 108-109
  materials 107
  overhead recovery 109
  of payables 107
  performance, see performance
    monitoring and control
  period 11
  points 90
  profits and balance sheet 91
  systems 13-14, 92
  world class manufacturing
    110-111
controllable costs 10, 90-91
controls (marketing plan) 50
Cook, I. 60, 112, 115
corporate level planning 22
corrective actions 99, 100

cost
  allocation analysis 139-140
  centres 9
  management process 112-116
  of reports 94
  targets 40-41
  and value of funds 79-80
  variance analysis 139
costs
  controllable 10, 90-91
  distribution 30
  fixed 25, 40, 64-66
  maintenance 29, 77
  marketing 30, 40, 49, 55
  new proposals 55
  operating 40
  other 31
  personnel 67, 131, 139
  production 71
  and productivity ratios 140
  programmed/managed 66
  repair and inspection 77
  sales force 69
  variable 25, 28-29, 40, 64-65
Coulthurst, N.J. 104
creditors 33-34, 132
cumulative figures (performance)
  95-96
current assets 32-33, 85
current liabilities 33-34, 85, 139
current taxation 34

deadlines, tasks and 130
debentures 35
debt-equity ratio 25
debt analysis, net 141
debtors 33, 132, 140
decentralisation 13
decision packages 113-114
deferred taxation 36
demand characteristics of markets
  46
demographic features 42
departmental objectives 26
deposits, cash and 33
depreciation 75-77, 83
development costs 55
differential advantage 43
direct labour productivity 110
discretionary marketing
  expenditure 29, 56, 138
distribution 30, 70
dividend cover 24, 136

dividends 34
downside sensitivity analysis 41, 56, 140
draft budget 14, 18
drilling down 92
duty, taxation and 28

earnings per share 24, 135
economic environment 59-60
economy (assessment) 64
effectiveness 64
efficiency 64, 69
employees
    cost 67, 131, 139
    numbers 67-68
    - related payments 68
engineering 29, 70, 131
equity, issue of 84
evaluation 2, 39
expenditure 90, 139
    operating and (budgets) 59-71
expenses 68, 139, 140
external factors (variance) 98
external trade creditors 33-34

factory operating budget 131-132
fashion chain 124-130
final budgets 18
finance leases 36
finance review 127
financial
    accounting controls 13-14
    appraisal 54
    budgets 21-22, 50
    objectives 8, 24-25, 135-136
    planning 22
    statements 54-55, 80-82, 84, 122
    year 124
financial objectives and budgets
    balance sheets 25-26, 31-32
    board's role 26
    budget guidelines 26-27
    financial planning levels 22
    marketing plans 22-23
    objectives 21, 23-26
    profit and loss 25-31
    statements 27
financing needs, long-term 34-35
finished goods inventory turnover 111
first half plans 125-126
first time sales 53
five year plans 55, 124-125

fixed assets 31-32, 75-76, 83-84, 132
fixed costs 25, 40, 64-66
flexible budgets 10, 12, 95, 97
flexible manufacturing systems 104-105
follow-up (corrective action) 100
food and drinks company 135-136
forecast variance summary 141
forecasts 96, 121
full year plans 125
functional objectives 26
funding requirements 85
funding targets 41
funds 79-80, 83, 132
funds flow
    budget period 86
    categories 82
    control 91
    profits and 79
    statements 80-84, 137, 140
    working capital budgets and 79-87

geographic distribution 42
global markets 44
goods and services 42
goodwill 31
Gordon, P.N. 60, 112, 115
government grants 84
gross margins 129
group budgets 16-19, 117-119
group creditors 34
group loans 36
growth 129
guideline budgets 14, 18

head office 18, 140
headcount 67, 69, 133
horizontal organisations 9
Hyndman, N. 112

improvements 77
income 31, 139
income budgets (preparation) 37-57
incoming quality 110
incremental budgeting 111
indirect productivity 111
industrial markets 42
information 2, 15, 94-95
inputs 60, 62-64
inspection costs 77

integrated control systems 13-14, 92
inter-firm comparisons 97
interest rate 132-133, 136
internal creditors 34
internal factors (variance) 98
international food and drinks
    company 135-136
inventory 111
investments 32, 49

just-in Time manufacturing
    106-110

knock-on effect on working capital
    86

labour 107-110, 131
    see also employees
leadership 5
    brand 49
liabilities 35-36
    current 33-34, 85, 139
liquidity 25
loans, group 36
long-run investment appraisal 49
long-term budgets 11, 33-35, 83-84,
    97-98, 121
'loss leaders' 53

maintenance costs 29, 77
managed fixed costs 66
management accountant (role) 3
management accounting 110
management information 2
managerial staff 68
manning levels 99
manufacturing costs 29
manufacturing lead times 110
margin analysis 25, 41, 56
market
    opportunities 39
    segments 42
    share 47, 56, 129, 141
    trends 17
marketing
    costs 30, 40, 49-55
    development 55
    expenditure 29, 56, 138
    mix 43-44
    objectives 23-24, 38, 50
    policy 43
    strategy 41, 50
    targets 39

markets 41-42, 44, 46-47
Maskell, B. 110
master budget 6, 12, 14, 114
material yield 111
materials 99, 107, 131, 139
medium-term budgets 11, 97
monetary sales 129
monitoring 63-64, 99-100, 130
monthly data 7, 126, 128, 137-140

natural business year 11
net debt analysis 141
net profits 41
net working capital 85
new assets 76-77
new products 45, 57, 103-104
new proposals 54-55
newspaper group 117-121
newspaper product prices 139
newspaper revenue 139
non-financial performance 99-100
non-trading provisions 83

objectives 2, 15, 17, 70, 94-95
    business 7-8, 23-24, 38, 135
    financial 8, 24-25, 135-136
    marketing 23-24, 38, 50
    operations 8, 61
    setting 26, 113
    see also financial objectives and
        budgets
open systems 61
operating
    budgets 12
    costs 40
    and expenditure budgets 59-71
    objectives 8, 61
operational comparisons 96-97
organisation structure 117
organisational objectives 24
organisational plan 38
outputs 60, 62-64
overall fixed costs 66
overdrafts 34
overhead budgets, JIT 109
overtime premiums 68

parent companies 16-17
past periods (performance) 96
pay rates 99
payables, control of 107
payment periods 25
payroll costs 139

performance
  control 89-95
  measures 110-111
  monitoring 2, 89-101, 115, 119, 126
  product 54
  review 127
personnel costs 67, 131
phased data 137-140
physical factor centres 10
place (marketing mix) 43
planning 7, 22, 124-126
prices 2, 40, 43, 48, 52, 56-57, 138, 140
pro forma statements 27
problems, budgeting 103-116
'product steal' 53
production 13, 55, 70-71, 106
productivity 110, 111, 140
products 26, 41-44, 49, 54
  life cycle 50-51
  market share 47, 56, 129, 141
  new 45, 57, 103-104
  sales targets 39-40
  viability 45-46
profit centres 9
profit and loss accounts 25-31, 137, 140-141
profit protection plans 19
profitability 24-25, 41, 57, 87, 138
profits 31, 41, 55, 79, 83, 91
programme budgets 12
programmed fixed costs 66
projected variance 96
promotion (marketing) 43, 52
prototype development 55
providers of funds 86
provisions 34
published company objectives 135
Phyrr, Peter 111

quantity 2

rate of return budget centres 9
rates 129-130
ratios and operational comparisons 96-97
raw-in-process category 107
recommended retail price 56
records of product performance 54
refurbishments 77
regional newspaper group 117-121
regional performance review 127

rents 129
repeat sales 53
replacement sales 53, 77
reports 6, 93-94, 99-100
resources 49, 115
responsibility accounting 12, 91-92
responsibility level 112-113
retail fashion chain 124-130
retail supermarket chain 121-124
return on assets 24, 136
revenues, controllable 10
review variances 94
revised drafts 18
reward systems 100-101
risk management 80
rolling budgets 11-12, 95

salaries 68-69, 99, 129, 139
sales 13, 25, 38, 53
  budgets 37, 131
  fixed assts 83-84
  force (costs of) 30, 69-70
  forecasts 131
  increases (per square foot) 129
  targets 39-40, 49
  volume 28, 48, 99
Schonberger, Richard 105
seasonal factors 11
second half plans 126
sector, volume and market share by 47
sensitivity analysis 41, 56, 140
service department budgets 12, 99
services 42, 44-45
short-term budgets 10, 34, 82-83, 98
Simmonds, K. 2
sociological characteristics 42
spares 53
specimen forms 137-141
standard cost up-date 134
starting time 16
statements 54-55, 80-82, 84, 122
statistics, key budget 133
stock levels 32-33, 131-132
stock ratios 25
stockbrokers 46
strategic budgets 2, 38
strategic plans 17
subsidiaries 17, 18, 32
supermarket chain 121-124
supplier-receiver reviews 113
supplies 99

supply characteristics of markets
46-47
SWOT analysis 43, 50
systems approach 60-61

tangible fixed assets 32
targets
    cost, asset and profit 40-41
    sales 39-40, 49
tasks 15, 94-95, 130
taxation 18, 24, 28, 34, 36,
132-133, 139
Texas Instruments 111
timeliness (reports) 93-94
timetable, see budget timetable
timing effects on working capital 87
top down approach 121
total quality control 105-106
trade creditors/debtors 132
trade investment 32
trade plan 38
trading budget 132
traditional management accounting
110
transfer pricing 57, 140
treasury function 18, 80

unit variable costs 64-65

values 2, 40-41, 79-80
variable costs 25, 28-29, 40, 64-65
variances 94, 98-99, 141
VAT 28
vendor leadtime 111
vertical organisations 9
volumes 40, 47-48, 70-71

wages 68-69, 99, 129, 139
work-in-progress 107, 110
working capital 74-75, 79-81, 84-87
world class manufacturing 105,
110-111

zero-base budgeting 111-112,
114-116